DAD SCARES ME, GOD SCARES ME

My Journey from Polygamist Cult to Freedom

Vera LaRee

Watermark Publishing
Colorado, USA

Dad Scares Me, God Scares Me:
My Journey from Polygamist Cult to Freedom
A Memoir by Vera LaRee

Cover Photo: Vera LaRee | Age 16 | Wedding Photo

Published by Watermark Publishing
Colorado, USA
www.watermarkbookpublishing.com

This is a work of nonfiction and although it is a true account of the author's life, except for major locales and certain public figures, all individuals' names and many identifying details have been changed.

Library of Congress Cataloging-in-Publication Data
LaRee, Vera
    Dad scares me, God scares me / Vera LaRee. – 1st ed.
        1. Title. 2. Memoir. 3. Polygamy. 4. Cult Life.

ISBN 978-1-938984-29-7 (Paperback)
ISBN 978-1-938984-30-3 (eBook)

First U.S. Edition: February 2020
First International Edition: February 2020

To my mother, the bravest woman I know.
Even though you are no longer on this earth,
your desire to put a smile on every face and a song
in every heart lives on through me and
all of your children. I love you!

CONTENTS

INTRODUCTION

I grew up in different parts of Mexico, all of which were selected by my father's prophet to be holy places. Places where God's people were to do a great work.

My father was a Caucasian, medium-framed, bald headed man. He was quite good looking and always dressed like a cowboy. Sharp-toed boots and cowboy hats along with fancy belt buckles and freshly pressed, button-down shirts would charm any young girl when accompanied by his smile.

A man with a mission, my dad joined the Saunders cult long before I was born, and the ideas and principles that our prophet, Jerome Saunders, taught were deeply embedded in his belief system. He took the prophecies and the words of Jerome to be the direct words of God.

Jerome Saunders declared himself a prophet, ordained by his father, A.D. Saunders—who claimed to have had a vision about Mexico and the United States after being dissatisfied with the LDS Mormon Church. In this vision he saw the destruction of the United States, horrified by blood running through the streets, calamities, famine, and the merciless suffering of millions of people—watching as the flesh fell off their bones causing them to cry out in agony. He claims to have asked God to shut the vision off because he couldn't stand the gruesome details of such horrific suffering.

He was then shown a vision of a flourishing Mexico. Land being tilled, orchards planted, and an abundance of honey and cattle. He witnessed people being educated and schools and businesses thriving. He was told by God to take his family to Mexico and to never let them go back over the old trail to the United States. My father believed in this vision fervently and he was adamant about teaching his children to believe in it as well. And, although Jerome Saunders was murdered by his own brother when I was just over a year old, his doctrine was taught in our home, in our church, and in our community.

Living polygamy, never going back to the United States and the belief that this was the only true church of God on the face of the earth were all part of this doctrine. And until the day he died, my father believed that Jerome and his father, A. D. Saunders, were true prophets—never letting go of the belief that God would eventually send another prophet to take their place.

***

Special Note: Out of respect for their privacy, the first and last names of my family members, friends, and all others who were part of my cult experience (both living and deceased), have been changed in this Introduction and in the pages that follow.

—Vera LaRee

PROLOGUE
January 15, 2013

As I make my way into the church and sit next to a group of my siblings, I wonder how many of my fifty-seven brothers and sisters will be here, and how many of his eleven wives I will see.

At the front of the church, I see a casket with dozens of flowers surrounding it. It is made of a special raw pine—its cover open, displaying the final destination of one man's journey. From where I am sitting, I cannot see the face inside the coffin, but I can see a pair of silent hands, resting—one on top of the other—as if death were a holy accomplishment; the last rung on the ladder for a man who never stopped climbing. Quietly, I stare at the lifeless hands—hands that I would recognize anywhere. They are the hands of my father, the man who gave me life but took away my freedom to live it by filling me with the dire consequences of not practicing his religious belief system—which included polygamy, otherwise known as celestial marriage.

Glancing around the room, I search for the face of only one other man. A man, like my father, who robbed me of my freedom by way of the same religion. This man, my late sister's husband and the father of my children, sits stoically in the back of the church. As my eyes find him amongst the last row of mourners, a rush of familiar emotion sizzles through my veins: Fear. Blazing Fear. Fear that set fire to my innocent heart, turning love into ashes.

It has been ten years since I've faced either of these men, and although one of them is dead, I'm not sure I am strong enough to withstand being in the same room with them again… Being back in Mexico—in this church and around these people—ignites hundreds of deep, dark memories. Memories of a life that I now wonder how I endured.

CHAPTER ONE

THE HOLY PLACE OF WEDDING SONGS & GANGSTERS

If Baja, Mexico was a holy place, then I was quite sure that anywhere less holy was not a place I wanted to spend eternity. If God's angels lived in crumbling houses with tattered sheets dividing the rooms and five-gallon buckets of poop waiting to be carried to the outhouse every morning, then the house of the devil was not a house I ever wished to visit. So, I did what I was taught; what I was told, what was expected of me—believing it was the only way to save myself from eternal damnation. After all, if this was Heaven, then what must hell be like?

"Do you like it, Vera?" asked my fifteen-year-old half-sister, Amy—holding up the bodice of the white, satin wedding dress she was making.

Sitting on a wooden chair with an old Singer sewing machine on a table in front of her, she looked so excited. Preparing for her wedding, just around the corner, gave her a golden glow as she held the smooth fabric in her hands and smiled at me.

Although it wasn't quite finished yet, I thought the dress was beautiful and tried to imagine how happy she must feel. Even though I was only seven, I knew I would be getting married some-day, too—but hoped it would *not* be to someone with as many wives as my father had.

"Yes, I do," I replied, gazing at the dress. "It's beautiful."

"Pretty soon you'll be making your own wedding dress," she said, slipping the white satin underneath the needle again and push-ing the sewing pedal with her foot. The old machine made a gentle humming sound and as Amy gently pulled the material through the feed head, I stood looking at her face.

She's so pretty, I thought... Her blonde hair and green eyes matched mine, but I never saw her as I saw myself. Her smile was so warm, and when she spoke her eyes sparkled. She always seemed to be happily working on one project or another—baking, sewing, or making crafts—it didn't matter what it was, she did it with joy; and I knew she was going to be a good wife.

Happy as I was for her, I suddenly felt a sadness welling up in my heart. Remembering that her wedding day was getting closer and she would no longer be living near us, I struggled with my con-trasting feelings. In my mind, her marriage looked like an elegant olive tree casting an exotic shadow... So beautiful when viewed from one angle—nothing but golden sunlight dancing with leaves. But viewed from another angle, it became a long, lonely path of darkness—the shadow-side of an otherwise glorious day.

I loved her so much and wished she wasn't moving away after her wedding but, of course, she would—because that's the way things were. You get married. You go where your husband wants you to go. You live where he tells you to live. For all his wives, the man always decides.

I had only met Samuel, the man she was going to marry, a few times. He seemed nice, although I didn't really know much about him. I tried to recall exactly what he looked like.

The Singer machine stopped humming. Amy looked up at me. "What are you thinking about?" she asked, adding, "You look a little sad."

"I was just thinking about Samuel. How do you know you want to marry him? I mean, he seems nice, but how do you know for sure?"

"Well," she answered, "I just know... The first time I met him, I asked him for a ride home from the beach. During that ride home, I felt a very strong connection to him and, somehow, I knew I would be marrying him. After I got out of his truck and closed the door, he rolled the window down to say good night. I looked at him, and without the slightest hesitation I told him I was going to marry him someday."

She smiled as she recalled that memorable moment, adding with certainty, "I love him so much, Vera, and I know I'm doing the right thing by marrying him."

Mama Louise, Amy's mom, poked her head into the room. "Vera, it's time to go," she said. "Practice starts in five minutes and your mom is going to be waiting for you."

I quickly gave Amy a hug. "I want you to make my wedding dress for me someday," I said, waving goodbye.

Not wanting to be late, I hurried along the dirt roads—passing Mama Nadine's house on my way home and seeing my half-sister, Bonita, outside. "Are you coming to practice?" I asked, quickly adding, "My mom is waiting for us. The wedding is in two weeks and she wants us to know all the words to the song she wrote for Amy and Samuel."

"I'll be right there," said Bonita.

Mama Nadine's house was across the olive field from ours and I was home in minutes. The huge tree in our front yard swayed in the breeze—its moving-shadows looked like monsters creeping along the cement walls of our house. There was no walk leading to the front door, only dirt, and as I stepped into the front room, I could see the back of Mom's figure. She held a book in one hand, while her other hand moved gracefully through the air.

Mom had chocolate-brown hair she kept in a braid, reaching half-way down her back. Her skin was lightly freckled, and she had small, brown eyes that matched her tiny button nose. She was a me-dium-sized woman, but it was hard to tell because she was always pregnant. (She had thirteen children for my father—seven sons and six daughters; me being her sixth child.) As her hand glided through the air, many of Dad's children close to my age—but from different wives—were singing: *Amy, Amy, do you have to go? We all will miss you so. Samuel, won't you let her stay?* Hurrying to the back of the room, I took my usual place—between my half-brother, Darryl, and Bonita's empty spot—and began to sing along.

Bonita was Mama Nadine's oldest child out of ten, and Darryl was Mama Louise's seventh child out of fifteen. The three of us were born within weeks of each other and, although we each had a different mother, we felt like triplets. We were in the same grades in school and in the same classes in church together, which made us feel uniquely connected with each other.

As practice went on, I couldn't help but notice that Bonita wasn't there yet. I wondered if her mom had made her stay home to clean or babysit again... Poor girl, I thought. She always has to work so hard.

As soon as practice was over and Mom had dismissed everyone, I walked back through the olive orchard to see why Bonita hadn't joined us. As I made my way through the trees and across the deep furrows used to irrigate, I knew I'd better hurry before Mom noticed I was gone. I dashed through the rose garden in the front yard and, after knocking on Mama Nadine's door and hearing Bonita yell for me to come in, I found her at the table feeding her mom's baby scrambled eggs... They looked so good. I couldn't remember the last time I'd had eggs—which were always a treat in our house, not part of our daily diet but reserved for the babies or for baking on special occasions.

"Why didn't you come to practice?" I asked Bonita.

"Because I had to watch the kids for my mom. She said she'd be right back, but she's still not here."

As if she had been called home by her daughter's words, Mama Nadine walked through the door. She had long, thick, black hair—the same color as her eyes—always pulled back into a neat braid that reached her waist. Her skin was a beautiful dark-olive color, and she was short like Dad's other Mexican wives. And, in perfectly broken English, she often shared stories with us—which we all loved!

As I sat with Bonita at the dining room table, I stared at the enormous black splotch above the front door. It looked like a dark secret had left its mark on the wall—stretching from the door frame to the ceiling.

"What is that black stuff above your front door?" I asked Mama Nadine, turning my head toward her.

She bent down and scooped up the baby from Bonita's lap, then sat down with him on the living room couch. "That," she said, "is from when the Adenites attacked this town a few years ago. They threw hand grenades through the windows and onto the roof, which set our house on fire. Luckily, it was put out before the whole house burned down. Nobody in this house was killed, but other members were not as lucky. In the other houses that went up in flames, two people were killed, and thirteen others were injured."

"Who are the Adenites?" I asked.

"They are really bad people," she warned. "Our prophet, Jerome, has a brother named Aden, who also wanted to be a prophet. After fighting with Jerome, he left to start a church of his own, taking some of his followers with him. He now claims to be the one al-mighty prophet and has committed several murders in the name of God, including the murder of our prophet—his own brother, Jerome. We have been told there is a list of members from our church who he's planning to kill, including your dad. We call Aden and the followers who have helped him commit murders the Adenites."

"My dad? Why does he want to kill my dad?"

"Because your dad doesn't believe in him and refuses to follow him."

"Do you think they'll come back and attack us too?"

"They might," said Mama Nadine, shrugging her shoulders.

Her words made my entire body shudder with fear… I didn't like the Adenites. I didn't like them one bit. And, knowing they might come back and kill us all at any time was a scary thought—one that stayed with me for a very long time.

I never felt the same after that conversation. Every time I was at Bonita's house and saw the eerie black splotch above the door, I was reminded of how unsafe I felt. I could not hear the name Aden without going into panic-mode and I often woke up with nightmares about him. I would lay in bed, frozen with fear, wishing prophets didn't exist. Which, I surmised, might leave Aden with no other choice than to be a better man—one who didn't ever want to do bad things to us.

Our home in Baja consisted of four adobe walls with a few windows. The inside was sectioned off with old, dingy sheets nailed to the wooden four-by-fours that supported the roof. We had no electricity, running water, or plumbing. There was a faucet sticking out of the wall in the kitchen with a sink which was supported by a wooden frame. No plumbing meant a bucket had to be placed underneath it to catch the water. Half the time it would spill over onto the floor and create a puddle before someone would notice that it needed to be emptied.

We had an outhouse we used during the day, and at night we kept a five-gallon bucket in the house which we called "the pot." We all had to take turns dumping the pot in the morning, and my prayer would always be that on my turn no one had gone poop during the night. Those emptyings were the worst! The smell was so bad it would make my stomach turn. I couldn't run to the outhouse with it fast enough! And, just when I thought the worst part was over, I would open the wooden door to the outhouse, pick the pot up to empty it and get sick to my stomach all over again as soon as I saw all the poop, flies and maggots at the bottom of the outhouse hole.

One evening, while sitting on the floor playing with my brothers, my mom walked in. She looked frightened as she quickly went around gathering kerosene, matches and lamps, along with a few blankets.

"Where is everybody?" she asked, nervously looking around the room. She hollered for the rest of the kids to come quickly, then bent down and spoke sternly but quietly to us all.

"The Adenites are coming!" she said frantically. "Mama Louise is coming to pick us up in Dad's truck and take us to our old house by the school. It's the farthest house from the entrance of town and we'll be safer there." Then she bravely straightened up, saying, "Come on. Let's go!"

I felt the fear creep up my spine… We're going to die, I thought. I don't want to die! I've been bad a few times and if I die, I will go to hell! "Please, Heavenly Father," I whispered, "if you keep us safe, I promise I'll be a really good girl! I'll do everything they teach me in Sunday school. Just please, God, don't let me die and go to the devil!"

"Vera, hurry!" my mom exclaimed, turning to look at me. "We've got to go!"

Mama Louise had already taken all of Dad's other wives and thirty-five of his children to our old house and we were the last trip which added another layer of tension to the responsibility of getting us all to safety. With the truck idling in front of our house, she quickly helped Mom load all the kids into the back of the truck then, looking nervous and scared, they both hopped in the front and we drove away.

The sun had set and all the houses we passed looked abandoned—not a single light shining from a window. It seemed that everyone had found somewhere else to go, anticipating the worst—yet still hoping for the best.

We pulled up behind our old house. Mom jumped out of the truck and herded us all through the front door. The rest of my brothers and sisters—same father, different mothers—were already inside and, just like me, they all stood in fear as Dad's wives spread blankets on the floor for the children to lay down on.

"Lay on your stomachs," we were instructed.

"Keep your hands to your sides and don't move!" Mama Nadine ordered.

"And please don't talk," said Mama Elaine.

Every child laid silently—backs to the ceiling—for what seemed like an eternity. Dad had left town, and I wondered why he had left us here knowing the Adenites were coming to kill us. It didn't seem right. I looked over at Mom just as she blew out the kerosene lamp—pitching us all into darkness. It was so quiet that I could hear myself breathing and I wondered if each breath would be my last as I waited for the Adenites to strike.

I must have fallen asleep waiting to die because the next thing I knew it was morning. After opening my eyes and looking around the room, I realized where I was and that I was not dead.

Most of those who had spent the night on the floor of our old house had already left, but Mom was sitting at a table with a few of Dad's wives. They spoke about how God had kept us safe—how He had kept the Adenites from attacking us. But in my heart, I knew it was because of my prayer to Him, and my promise to be good. It was my prayer and my promise that had kept us safe. I was sure of it.

CHAPTER TWO

RAISE YOUR HAND IF YOU WANT TO GO TO HEAVEN

In all religions, Heaven—to a seven-year-old—can be a tad confusing. Some children are told they are the chosen ones, which automatically makes them Heaven-worthy. They can steal, they can lie, they can disobey their parents, but they still get to go to Heaven. And then there are some, like myself, who are told they must marry their way there—and that scared the daylights out of me... What if no one wants to marry me? Or what if we run out of mush and I starve to death before I meet a boy? What then, I wondered... What happens to the girl who never makes it to the altar?

The following Sunday, I walked into the kitchen and saw that Dad had come home. Mom was busy serving her children breakfast—whole wheat mush with a little sugar sprinkled on top. Hardly a feast, but rarely did we have sugar, so we usually ate the mush topped with a pinch of salt. Dad's family was so large that it was all he could do to put food on the table for all of us, so no one complained—we just ate whatever was put in front of us, always thankful for a few grains of sugar.

I picked up a metal bowl—its chipped white coating dulled by years of use—and held it up so Mom could fill it with mush. "You need to eat quickly," she said, spooning mush into my bowl, "so we can make it to church on time."

I sat down on one of the two wooden benches flanking the sides of our long dining room table. It was old and ugly, but Mom covered it with a plastic tablecloth—its colorful flower pattern making the whole room seem a little brighter. The flowers camouflaged the countless drips and spills of small children, and when the chipped bowls were cleared away, it was easy to wipe clean. That was my mother's ever-ingenious and resourceful way of living—one plastic tablecloth, many perks.

I didn't want to go to church because my dad was going to be there and although it was normal for me to feel uneasy around him, I knew today would be worse. I was still upset with him for neglecting his fatherly duty of keeping us safe when the Adenites threatened to attack and kill us, but I knew there was no getting out of going to church.

Resigning myself to spending the day with my seemingly uncaring father, I gagged down the mush and asked to be excused. Back in my bedroom—with walls made of grungy sheets hanging from the rafters—I rummaged through the piles of dirty clothes looking for my cleanest dirty dress.

At our house, clean clothes were a novelty. With eleven kids, it was impossible for Mom to keep up with the laundry. Dad's first wife, Mama Vee, had electricity in her house—and she had a Maytag wringer washer which she shared with all Dad's wives. They each had one day a week to do their laundry at her house, but one day wasn't enough to keep up with such a large family; and I couldn't wait for the day we, too, had electricity. Recently, I'd overheard Mom talking to her friend about somebody wiring our house—and, oh, I hoped it would be soon! I even dared to dream of having a wringer washer with a clothesline and clothespins, just like Mama Vee had!

Mom was also getting ready for church and after washing my face, I took the hairbrush and a few pieces of string to her so she could do my hair. She carefully parted it down the middle and made two braids down the sides, using the string to tie the ends. When she was done, she quickly got my brothers and sisters ready, then we all walked the few blocks to Mama Vee's house—but we did not continue on to church as usual, instead Dad would be teaching us at Mama Vee's house today.

Along with electricity and a washing machine, Mama Vee had the nicest house of all Dad's wives. It had an inside bathroom, although the toilet was old-fashioned—like the ones in old mobile homes. It had a pedal you pushed with your foot to flush it, with a tank on the bottom that needed to be emptied when it got full. There was also a white bathtub I loved bathing in whenever I stayed with her. There were no old sheets hanging from the ceiling to divide the rooms, but real walls—white and smooth. Her house also had a kitchen with lots of cabinets, a sink, a refrigerator, and—most unusual for any house in this part of Baja—there was carpeting in her front room.

We all knew she was Dad's favorite wife, and I could see why. She was the kindest, most loving, warmhearted woman I had ever met—and all of Dad's wives and children seemed to love her as much as I did. She had a beautiful soul, and it was impossible not to feel the genuine love she shared with every one of us.

Dad's voice suddenly commanded the attention of everyone in the room. "Everybody settle down now," he instructed. "Find a spot for yourself on the couches or chairs, and you kids find a spot on the floor—we're going to get started."

When we were all settled, he called on one of his older sons to offer the opening prayer. We all closed our eyes, bowed our heads, folded our arms, and listened. "Dear Heavenly Father," he began, "thank you for gathering us together here…"

When the prayer had been said, Mama Vee sat down at the piano to play a hymn. (Among her many lovely things, she also had an upright piano that she'd inherited and greatly treasured.) Mom stood up to lead us through the song. It was one we sang quite often in Sunday school, *Hail to the Prophet Ascended to Heaven,* and we all sang along.

When the song was over, Mama Vee turned around and faced us while Mom quickly made her way back to her seat. Dad looked around the room, then began the Sunday class.

He used a lot of big words—most of which I did not under-stand—but what I did understand was that there are three degrees of glory in Heaven, which means there are three levels of Heaven you can reach. However, there is only one level in hell and if you don't keep the Ten Commandments, that's where you'll end up. Young as I was, I listened very carefully because I knew that one of the Ten Commandments was to obey your father and mother; and missing anything Dad said would be disobeying him—not a chance I was willing to take.

"Keeping the Ten Commandments will only get you to the low-est level of Heaven," Dad told us in a stern voice, "but if you love your neighbor as yourself, you will make it to the second level. Now, which one of you here only wants to make it to the second level?" Then, looking at one of my sisters he asked, "Do you, Mary?"

"No," she answered softly. "I want to go to the high level."

"How many of you here want to go to the highest level? Show me with a raise of hand if you want to go to the highest level."

We all raised our hands, including my father.

"Then you all must take the law of celestial marriage seriously, like I have," he said. "There is no other way to make it to the high-est level except through living this law. I have sacrificed my life for the sake of plural marriage (another way of saying celestial marriage). Our prophet, Jerome, talked about this before he was murdered, and it is one of his greatest teachings. It is a disgrace how so many people in this world don't believe in polygamy or in having large families," he continued. "The first commandment in the Bible says, 'Be fruitful, multiply and replenish the earth,' yet there are so many people, especially in the United States, who only want one or two kids. Do you know how sad that makes God feel? Those kinds of people are not very worthy."

As I sat on the floor listening to my father's words, I thought about Heaven… His vision of that holy place wasn't the same as the holy place we lived in—Baja, where God's people live and do great work. So, perhaps the Heaven on Earth and the Heaven in the sky were very different. In my mind, I pictured sidewalks of gold. No sickness or dilapidated houses like ours. Mountains of delicious food, like waffles and cookies. And legions of winged angels who loved me very much. Then I imagined hell… A red devil swinging a whip with needles attached to the end—long, sharp needles that sank deep into your skin as he counted out fifty lashes. I saw dark, evil spirits with blood dripping out of their gargantuan alien-eyeballs, which scared me so much that icy shivers ran down my spine.

Quickly, I turned my attention back to Dad, now talking about living the gospel he'd sacrificed his life to teach us, and how he was showing us the way back to Heaven. Right then and there, I vowed to live this law—no matter what it took. There was no other way for me to gain God's love and approval, which is the only thing that would keep me safe from hell.

Later that day, when we were back at home, I noticed how tired Mom looked. Her belly was getting bigger, and our old, raggedy, brown couch—covered with a blanket to hide the rips and tears—seemed to be the only comfortable place for her to sit. She was reading a book, and I could see that it was a romance novel, not a church book or Bible. I wondered what kind of stories were in a book like that and I was curious to know exactly what a romance novel was. My mother certainly seemed to enjoy them, and I knew she read a lot of them because when she finished each book, she cut the pages into squares, then placed them in a cardboard box in the outhouse where we all used them in place of bathroom tissue—and that box was always full.

It might have been a good time to ask about the mysterious books—Mom looked so relaxed as she sat there reading—but I had bigger questions.

"Mom?" I said, hoping I wasn't disturbing anything important.

"Yes, Vera," she said, putting the book down.

"If God wants us to have big families and a lot of kids, then why does Mama Vee only have five kids?"

Knowing I was always thinking about something, Mom smiled at me. "Mama Vee wanted to have a lot more children," she said, "but when she was pregnant with her sixth child, she got really sick and almost died. And, because it was dangerous for her to give birth again, the doctors made it so she couldn't have any more babies. After that, she decided that if she couldn't have any more children of her own, she would just let all the love in her heart flow out to your dad's other children… She was your father's first love and he had no intention of living polygamy when they married. But they were both converted by Jerome—and they both agreed to celestial marriage—and she has believed and stood by your dad's side no matter what."

I sat down beside Mom as she continued, "We all love Mama Vee very much and she loves all of us. It doesn't seem to be as hard for her to love everyone in our celestial family as it is for some of your dad's other wives. She's like a sister to me," she added, her eyes getting misty. "I know she will make it to Heaven even though she only has five kids."

I thought for a minute about what my mother had just said, and it made sense to me. Suddenly it was easy to see why Mama Vee was always so kind and loving to me, and I now understood why my father spent most of his time at her house. Maybe he feels bad for her, I thought. Maybe it's why he makes sure she has so many nice things. And maybe he loves her so much more than he loves my mom and the other wives because she has always been so loving to everyone. I want to be like her when I grow up, I decided. I want to be kind and loving and a good sister-wife, just like her!

Our family prayer meetings were held at Mama Louise's house every morning before school. All the wives and children were required to attend. It was in these meetings that I learned the most about what was required of me to make it to Heaven—a place I desperately wanted to go!

Every morning we would pray, my father would preach, then we would all sing hymns—and Dad's wives often came up with fun ideas and games we could play to learn the gospel principles. If we did well, we were rewarded with things like pancake breakfasts or our favorite American candy: Sugar Daddies.

Mom was always in charge of the music. Not only did she have a great appreciation for it, she was also incredibly gifted—from playing the piano to singing to songwriting, my mother had a talent for it all. And, wanting to show us just how valuable music could be, she came up with the idea that we would each memorize one of the Mormon hymns from our hymnbooks. We had two weeks to memorize each song and if we got it right, we would get two pesos. Well, two pesos for memorizing a hymn was an irresistible challenge—so many of us learned the hymns, every word, no mistakes. We no longer had to scratch the dirt looking for coins. Our pockets jingled with pesos and we felt blessed—until Dad nearly went broke, which put an end to the hymn-rewards and sent us back to the dirt looking for a coin.

Sometimes serious, sometimes fun, our morning prayer meetings were instrumental in helping me understand the religion of polygamy. Every day I learned more about what God expected from me, as well as what was expected from a man and a woman in celestial marriage. Women, being the lesser of the two sexes, were to be submissive to their husbands. Men were to marry as many young wives as possible and have as many children as they could. They were also responsible for guiding their families with a stern and firm hand into the Kingdom of Heaven. Women could not make it to Heaven on their own. Only by obeying their husbands, were they allowed to enter God's kingdom.

My father's audience dared not question what he taught. His children were to absorb this information, not have an opinion about it—so we all adhered to the rule of children being seen and not heard. We quietly accepted the teachings as God's Law—no questions asked. And, whenever my father told us to raise our hands if we wanted to go to the highest level of Heaven, I always raised mine—unaware that by doing so I was signing an unbreakable contract. Not with my Father in Heaven, but with my father on Earth—and not only was I giving him authority over my life, I was giving him my soul.

As each day passed, although I never talked about it, I found less and less of a distinction between Dad's children and his wives. Even though we served one purpose and his wives served another, both had to obey him; and the consequences of doing otherwise could be painful.

One afternoon, while I was outside playing, I saw Dad speeding down the dirt road in front of our house. Thick clouds of dust swirled around his pickup truck, making it hard for me to see who was in the truck with him; although, when I squinted my eyes, I was sure I saw Mama Elaine in the passenger seat—and it looked like she was physically fighting with my dad. I watched as the truck roared by Mama Elaine's house, disappearing into the billowing dust as it sped down the road.

The following morning at prayer meeting, I noticed that Dad had a big bruise in the shape of a bite mark on his forearm. I also noticed that Mama Elaine was not there. She was one of my father's Mexican wives. Petite and pretty, with shoulder length, jet-black hair—one side held back with a barrette—and pale skin that made her seem rather fragile.

As I was wondering where she might be, one of my younger brothers pointed to the bruise on my father's forearm and asked, "What happened to you right there, Dad?"

Dad put his hand over the mark and lightly chuckled as if he was embarrassed about it, then said, "Mama Elaine was misbehaving yesterday, so I had to put her over my knee and give her a hard spanking. She fought back and bit me on the arm. That was uncalled for, so I spanked her again to teach her not to disrespect her husband in that way."

I immediately recalled the crazy driving I had witnessed the day before, wondering if it had something to do with what Dad had just said. And even though I knew I should, I did not feel one bit sorry for him—instead, my heart went out to Mama Elaine. I felt sorry for her and at the same time, I was proud of her. After all the times I had watched my father spank my brothers and sisters, I felt that Mama Elaine had given him exactly what he deserved.

CHAPTER THREE

BUT MOSTLY I CRIED FOR MY MOTHER

Struggling with what felt right and what did not was a useless endeavor. For the children of polygamy, to listen and obey paves the path to Heaven, and I had promised God that I would meet Him there no matter what I had to do—and, in turn, He had promised to love me. So, to silence the whisperings of my soul and to believe what I was told to believe seemed the right thing to do—or perhaps it was the only thing to do, because my soul did not belong to me. It belonged to my father.

One evening, while I was eating with a few of Mom's other children, she suddenly burst through the front door announcing that Dad had called an important family meeting. We were all supposed to meet in the front yard—five minutes ago.

Oh boy, I thought… Dad would not be calling a meeting at this hour unless something serious was going on. Hesitating before speaking, because I knew I'd be in trouble for questioning anything Dad told us to do, I quietly asked, "What for, Mom?"

"Your dad found out that your brothers, Ted and Daniel, took some quarters from Rudolfo's house," she said, giving me a worried look. "And he wants to talk to all of us about it."

I knew that Rudolfo had gone to the United States and my brothers were keeping an eye on his house while he was away. Other than that, I didn't know anything—and I couldn't help but wonder why my dad wanted all of us there... We hadn't taken any quarters!

Too anxious to finish the slice of bread I was eating, I jumped up from the table, ran outside—the others right behind me—and found Dad's large family gathered together. My brothers and sisters, along with Dad and his wives, had formed a circle. Four small, wooden chairs had been placed in a row at the front of the circle. Dad was already talking, but I managed to figure out exactly what was going on with his final words, "Ted and Daniel have stolen. Darryl and Sam did not steal, but they knew about the older ones stealing and didn't tell on them. This makes them just as guilty. I want all of you here to help me punish them so you will never forget what happens to us when we don't obey God's laws." Then, holding up a brown leather belt—its enormous silver buckle gleaming as it swung from his hand—he added, "I'm going to pass this belt around to each of you. The four brothers will bend over and place their hands on the backs of the chairs, and you will each take a turn whipping them."

This was the cruelest thing I had ever been asked to do, but I knew if I didn't do it—if I disobeyed my father—I would receive a punishment far greater. Completely horrified, I watched as each of my siblings took the belt, stood behind the brothers, and whipped them as hard as they could.

One of Mama Elaine's sons seemed to think the whole thing was funny. He laughed wickedly as he grasped the belt and mercilessly flogged their backsides—as if he were trying to slay dragons instead of reprimanding a couple of boys for stealing quarters and reminding the others, whose only crime was not tattling, that withholding the sins of your brothers makes you a sinner too.

I didn't understand what was so funny about my brothers gripping the backs of the chairs, crying out in pain. Cautiously, I looked over at Mom—hoping to draw courage from her. My turn was coming up soon and the thought of inflicting pain on my brothers was more than I could endure.

Mama was pregnant again and had one arm resting across the top of her belly and the other one underneath her chin. I could see the tears running down her cheeks as she stood, helpless, watching her sons being beaten. Dad, standing next to her, leaned a little closer—but instead of consoling her, I heard him say, "Stop being such a baby, Patrice."

My whole body cringed. My heart wept for my brothers, and for myself, but mostly it wept for my mother—unable to do anything to comfort her sons. Suddenly, I had an idea: When it was my turn to whip them, I'd just tap them lightly with the belt. That way, I wouldn't be inflicting pain on them or on my mother's heart.

The belt slowly made its way around the circle, and then it was my turn. Taking a deep breath, I walked up to the chairs and quickly tapped each brother's backside with the belt. But before I got back to my place in the circle, my father's stern voice cut through the air, "You go back and whip them again. You barely tapped them!"

In anguish, I almost fell to my knees. They were my brothers and I didn't want to hurt them… What kind of God would want me to whip my own brothers? And what kind of father would ask me to do such a thing? I did not understand where cruelty and violence fit into the holy plan that the adults surrounding me always talked about. I didn't understand any of it. But if I disobeyed my father, I would be breaking one of the Ten Commandments which would make God very sad.

Slowly, I walked back to the first of the four brothers, grit my teeth, and swung the belt. When the leather met his already burning backside, a torrent of tears gushed from his eyes as he cried out in pain. My heart begged me to throw the belt on the ground and walk away, but I couldn't—I wanted to, but I didn't know how to stop what felt so wrong.

Choking back my own tears, I stood behind the second brother. My resolve to be a good girl—to do everything I was told to do and never disobey my father—was quickly crumbling; and I was crumbling with it. A sob rose from my soul and into the air as the belt came down on the backside of another brother.

Finally, I stood behind the last one—the youngest of the four. His small hands clung to the back of the chair waiting for another searing slap of leather—his tears turning into slime as they mixed with the snot dripping from his nose; all of it running down the back of the chair. I raised the belt, his little face turned toward mine. "I love you," I mouthed to him, as the belt of my father wailed across his backside.

Desperate to let go of the belt, I ran back to the circle, handed it to my sister, then turned around—facing away from the others; wanting, more than anything, to sink into my mother's arms. My tears wouldn't stop—I felt so alone, so scared.

Daring to turn my head and glance up at her, I saw that Mom was still crying—probably feeling just as alone and as scared as me. Had I not been so terrified of what my dad might do to us, I would have run to her, I would have hugged her, and I know she would have hugged me. But we were both trapped in the same world—the holy place, where God's people beat their children.

I don't understand God's laws, I thought—still looking at her. But I'm afraid to break them. I'm afraid of disobeying my fathers—both of them; the one who lives in Heaven and the one who lives on Earth. I cannot disobey either of them.

I was so confused—nothing felt right. My brothers were still sobbing. My mother's face was drenched with tears. My heart felt like it was breaking. And the only thing I knew for sure was this: Dad scares me, God scares me.

CHAPTER FOUR

PELTED WITH ROCKS; HAUNTED BY HUNGER

Hunger is a vicious master. It can turn innocent children into sinners—not because they steal food, but because those with the food have the power to steal the innocence of the child.

Walking home from school on a sweltering afternoon, I tugged at the yellow pinafore that kept sliding backwards—cutting into my neck, making it hard to breathe—perilously close to choking me. Frustrated by the heat and the pinafore, I tried to keep my mind on better things… a cool breeze, clothes that fit properly, our long table—covered with a plastic tablecloth—heaped with delicious food. But instead of making me feel better, just thinking about food made my stomach growl.

Hunger haunted me. I was sure I could eat a horse, and equally sure that supper would be yet another bowl of boiled beans. Served in a chipped bowl.

Suddenly, something hit the back of my head. It felt like a rock, and it hurt so much that I yelped in pain. Wincing, I gently pressed the palm of my hand against the sore spot, feeling something sticky oozing from my head. Alarmed, I looked at my fingers, now covered with blood. As I turned to see who had pelted the rock at me, another one whizzed by—barely missing my face before landing in the dirt.

Squeezing my eyes shut, I lowered my chin and fought back the tears. Even though he had attacked me from behind, I was sure I knew who the rock-thrower was, and I didn't want him to see me cry. Feeling warm blood trickling down my back, I lifted my head and got a good look at the boy whose house I had just passed—confirming the identity of the culprit. His arm swung back, then forward, as he hurled another rock my way, yelling profanities in Spanish.

Dodging the flying rock, I turned around and ran toward home—hearing more rocks showering the road behind me. Finally stopping to catch my breath when I felt a safe distance away, I touched the back of my head again. Sticky blood was still oozing from the wound, so I kept going—heading for home as quickly as I could, thinking about the boy who hurled rocks at little girls… His name was Javier. He was one of the two Saunders-Otero boys. Their Mexican mother, now the ex-wife of Samuel's polygamist father, Victor, was jealous of his American wives and had eventually left him.

Jolted out of my thoughts by the sight of Dad's brown pickup parked on the road in front of our house, I stopped. He seemed to like to park there, or in the front yard, but he rarely got out of his truck. He just stayed in the driver's seat while Mom sat in the passenger seat, and sometimes they sat there for hours.

Only occasionally did my father come inside the house which I always thought was because there were so many kids—lots of noise, growling stomachs, piles of dirty clothes everywhere. Our house wasn't clean and quiet like Mama Vee's, nor did we have the conveniences she had. But part of me was glad he rarely came inside because when he was there, I felt afraid—and I didn't like feeling afraid.

Not about to bother him, or my mother, I went around to the water tap at the back of the house. A slimy puddle of mud surrounded the outdoor tap, but I managed to stretch out my arms and turn it on without sliding into it. Letting the water run into my cupped hands, then dousing myself with it, I did my best to wash the blood out of my hair and off my neck.

Hearing the door of Dad's truck slam shut, followed by the gentle footsteps of my mother, I turned around.

"Vera, what happened to you?" Mom asked.

"Somebody threw a rock at me," I said, filling my hands with water again and pouring it over my head.

"Let me see," she said, leaning over me and separating my hair with her fingers. "It looks like a puncture wound that got you right on a vein. You'll be all right. Who threw the rock at you?"

"It was Javier, Mom… Why is he always so mean to us? I didn't do anything to him."

"Well, their mother had a hard time living polygamy with Victor and all his wives. After she left him, she became very bitter towards whites, especially women. I think she has taught her children to be bitter towards them as well. Just try to be forgiving, Vera. It's not their fault that their mother is teaching them hatred. She never really had the gospel in her."

I'll be forgiving, I thought, but I'll never again pass by their house when I'm walking home from school! From now on I'll take the longer way around, which means I'll have to cut through the backyard of one of the members of our church. Suddenly my heart groaned, remembering the last time I had cut through that yard…

It was a cloudy afternoon. Mom had asked me to run to the small grocery store in town and buy some sugar… Two of my younger brothers went with me. As we were crossing the church member's front yard, I noticed a white station wagon with brown stripes parked in the driveway. A man whom I had never seen before sat in the passenger seat with the door wide open. He was a heavy-set man with black hair. And, although he was wearing dark-rimmed glasses, I could see his unkempt, bushy eyebrows. His face was full of deep wrinkles and the hair on his arms was an ugly tangle of black and gray. I thought he might be one of the men that my friend, Vivian, had told me about... Her dad was another brother of our prophet, Jerome—and he also believed he held some sort of priesthood. He often brought back strange people from the United States who he was trying to convert, so I assumed this man must be one of those people.

The man was eating a big, red apple—a delicacy in my world! I watched as he put it up to his mouth to take another enormous bite out of it. My mouth watered as I imagined its sweetness, and an overwhelming desire to have one came over me.

"Hello there," said the strange man.

Hesitantly but politely, my brothers and I returned his greeting.

"Whatcha doing?" he asked, setting the half-eaten apple on the dashboard, then reaching for something behind him.

Without answering him, I put an arm around each of my brothers' shoulders and gently urged them to keep going—but the man continued talking. "Come here for a minute," he said, as we started walking away.

We all stopped and turned around. "Would you three like some of these?" the man asked, holding out a big plastic bag full of apples.

My brothers' eyes lit up and before I could stop them, they raced back to the man, plunged their hands into the bag—each grabbing an apple—then began devouring the delicious fruit we often dreamed about, but rarely ever had.

As I watched them thoroughly enjoying every bite, the man looked at me. "Aren't you going to have one?" he asked, holding the bag out to me.

I could smell the apples from where I was standing. I could taste them just by watching my brothers bite through the crisp, red skin; sinking their teeth into the luscious fruit—smiling with every bite.

Slowly, I walked over and reached into the bag, then suddenly the man grabbed my arm. Frozen in fear, I just stood there as the man's eyes ran up and down my body—stopping at my lips. "You can have this whole bag," he said, with an eerie grin, "but first you have to give me a kiss."

Gross, I thought—not daring to move—I'm not doing that! But my mind quickly went back to the apples, remembering how delicious they were and how much I wanted one. And, for a second, I silently reconsidered his offer. Just one quick little kiss in exchange for a whole bag of apples?... Apple pie, apple cake, apples, apples, apples.

Feeling his rough grip tighten around my arm, I pushed my thoughts away—cautiously looking at the man again. His bushy eyebrows and the long hairs sticking out of his nose were disgusting, and I knew I could never kiss him no matter what he offered me! I hated the way his probing eyes made me feel—roving up and down my body—and I suddenly didn't care about having an apple. I just wanted to get away from him!

"No, thank you," I said quietly, trying to pull my arm away. But my struggle only made him hold on tighter and, yanking me up against him—crushing the bag of apples between us—he placed his slobbery mouth over mine.

My mind reeled as his tongue pressed hard against my lips—his rank saliva dripping down my chin. Horrified, I squeezed my lips together as tight as I could—knowing that what he was doing was wrong. Dreadfully wrong. The little voice inside myself urged me to flee, but I couldn't free my arm from his iron grip, and his vulgar tongue kept trying to force its way into my mouth no matter how hard I tried to push him away.

Desperate to be free from the horrible man, my heart let out a helpless whimper. Then, just as suddenly as he had grabbed me, he let me go—giving me a sleezy smile as he adjusted the front of his pants and handed me the bag of apples.

Grabbing the bag, I turned around and fled. My brothers had already dashed across the front yard without me and, quick as lightening, they were running toward the path that wound through the weedy grove of trees behind the house—the shortcut to the store. Hugging the bag of apples, I flew like the wind—trying to catch up with them and with my own feelings as well.

As we quickly made our way to the store, I kept thinking about the awful man—asking myself over and over why he had done what he'd done; knowing that none of it was right yet wondering if it was what men were supposed to do to girls. And, although something deep within me sensed something very negative, I managed to dismiss the feeling by remembering what I had been taught: Men are superior to women. They have the right to do whatever they want to do, even if the woman doesn't like it. Men are to be obeyed. And if any woman strays from that teaching, she'll never get to Heaven.

So, I concluded, maybe when I'm older it will be different. Maybe a man trying to force his tongue into my mouth won't seem so disgusting—or so scary.

This was the first time of many that I reasoned myself away from my internal guidance system—giving more value to what I had been taught than to what my heart knew was true.

CHAPTER FIVE

SMILES AND TEARS

Within me, live two little girls. One wears her brother's old, raggedy clothes—and smiles while she sings. The other wears a pretty dress—and quietly weeps instead of singing. Their older sister stands between them, one girl holding her right hand—the other holding her left. What these two little girls have in common is that they both love holding their sister's hand; although, when it's time for her to leave them, the girl in the ragged clothes does not know how to hang on, and the girl wearing the pretty dress does not know how to let go.

The unmistakable aroma of something delicious wafted through the air. Jumping out of bed, I ran to the kitchen where I found Mom removing a tray of cookies from the oven. It was my birthday, but I hadn't expected anything special, so I wasn't sure they were for me… With a spatula, Mom gently lifted the cookies from the tray and placed them on the table to cool.

"What are the cookies for?" I asked, noticing that the whole table was full.

"They're for your birthday," she said. "There's one cookie for each of your dad's children and I'm going to pass them out to everyone after prayer meeting this morning. And, if we have enough time, maybe we'll all sing to you."

Because it was my birthday, I wondered if there was a way for me to have two, but I knew better than to ask. Cookies were not something we had very often. Dad's already large family was constantly getting bigger; and with so many wives and children to feed, Mom received only a tiny allowance to feed us—and she always bought the same things: Beans, potatoes, wheat. Salt, yeast, lard. And a little sugar, when she could afford it... Combining these few ingredients in creative ways was a challenge, but Mom did the best she could with what she had and, somehow, managed to keep us all fed.

"Happy birthday!" said Mom, sliding the last tray of cookies into the oven. Then, sitting down on the bench, she carefully placed the cooled cookies into a large bowl.

I could hear her counting under her breath, making sure she had enough for everyone. "Perfect," she said, when she finished counting. "Exactly enough! Now hurry and wake the rest of the kids so they can get ready for prayer meeting and school. And, sweetie, you get ready, too, but you don't have to wear your school uniform today."

"Why?" I asked, a little confused because we were never allowed to attend school in regular clothes.

"Because today you get to skip school," Mom said, smiling. "Mama Louise is going to take you for a little ride for your birthday, and I'm letting you miss school for that."

A cookie, skipping school, *and* a birthday ride? My heart danced with joy—I felt so special even if I didn't get to have a birthday party, with a cake and presents, like my friend, Vivian. This was infinitely better than anything I could have hoped for, and I was incredibly excited!

I hurried back to the room where my brothers and sisters were sleeping and woke them. "Mom said to get up and get ready for prayer meeting and school!" I hollered as I began looking for my purple and white dress—the special one that I only wore on Sundays. But, not finding it in the stack of clean clothes, I began digging through the pile of dirty clothes. Finally locating my dress and carefully examining it, I knew it was too dirty to wear on this special day, so I went back to the little stack of clean clothes—finding only a pair of stained jeans and a dark green T-shirt that belonged to one of my brothers. Oh well, I thought, today is going to be a special day even if I have to wear my brother's clothes again. (Being born in the middle of five boys, I had to wear their clothes a lot but, even though I would have loved wearing pretty clothes, it really wasn't such a big deal.)

After dressing, I found the brush and string, then rushed back to mom to get my hair done. She had finished the baking and was now getting ready to go to our prayer meeting. She did my hair in braids, then told me to head over to Mama Louise's house.

Happily, I skipped all the way there—so excited I thought I might burst. "Knock, knock!" I shouted, standing outside the front door.

"Come in," said Mama Louise's oldest daughter, Amy—one of my favorite half-sisters—as she placed another log into the wood-burning stove. She had her hair scooped up in a ponytail and was wearing jeans and a green shirt like me. Although her jeans were her own and her shirt was a lighter shade of green than mine, we both smiled because we were wearing the same colors.

"Look at that," she said. "We're dressed like twins!"

Together, we laughed at the notion of being twins, then she added, "It's your birthday today. Happy birthday!"

"Thank you," I said. "Your mom is going to take me for a birthday ride!"

"She is? Are you excited?"

"Yes!"

"I'm excited, too," she said. "It's not my birthday, but it's almost my wedding day!"

Oh, that, I thought... Although I had been to practice and had learned every word of the special song we would be singing to her and Samuel, I tried not to think about her leaving.

As I leaned against the dining room table, she put the last piece of wood into the stove. Then, turning around with a concerned look on her face, she asked, "Aren't you excited for me?"

"I am," I answered. "But I'm going to miss you. Mom said you're going to live in Chihuahua and I'll never get to see you anymore."

Amy put her arm around my shoulder. "Don't be sad, sis, I'll be back to visit and besides, maybe Dad will decide to move the family over there too. Most of Jerome's people live there, and I overheard Dad talking to Mom about possibly moving back someday."

Putting her hand under my chin and raising it up, she added, "Cheer up, it's your birthday today! No more sadness."

Wrapping my arms around her, I hugged her tight, loving that she hugged me back... Although there was a seven-year gap in our ages, I always felt that she understood me—like we were on the same wavelength. I felt so proud to be her sister; we had such a unique bond, one that I had never experienced with any of my other sisters.

The family began arriving for our prayer meeting as I made my way into the front room. I sat down on one of the little wooden school chairs and waited for Mom to arrive with the cookies.

After the meeting was over and everyone sang *Happy Birthday,* Mom passed out the cookies. Mine tasted so good—I chewed slowly, letting it melt in my mouth, thoroughly enjoying every bite.

"Are you ready to go for a birthday ride?" Mama Louise asked, as the rest of the kids hurried off to school.

"Yes," I answered, popping the last piece of cookie into my mouth.

"Then run and hop in the truck," she said. "I'll be there in a minute."

I felt a little nervous about having so much attention lavished on me—but at the same time, it felt wonderfully exciting. A few minutes later Mama Louise hopped in the driver's seat and away we went. She drove me up and down the roads in our little town, then stopped at the small grocery store. I waited for her in the truck as she dashed inside, quickly returning with a single yellow banana in her hand. She smiled as she handed it to me. "Here you go, Vera," she said. "Happy Birthday!"

A sweet, ripe banana all to myself for my birthday, I thought, and I don't have to share it with my younger siblings... I felt so special!

We drove down a few more roads before she took me home, and before I jumped out of the truck, I gave her a radiant smile. "Thank you, Mama Louise," I said, speaking straight from the center of my heart. "I had the best birthday ever!"

***

I could feel the excitement in the air as the sun streamed through the church windows. From my place in the second row, I had an unobstructed view of the wall behind the podium which was decorated with light-blue crepe paper streamers that had S + A written on them, meaning: Samuel plus Amy.

Samuel stood in front of the podium facing the guests as they took their seats. He was a handsome groom—tall and thin, with bluish-green eyes. His hair was blonde and slightly wavy in the front. He had sideburns and a slight mustache—which somehow made his front teeth look small, although it certainly didn't make him any less attractive.

When he and his friends and family had gathered in our front yard yesterday—right after they'd arrived for the wedding—I noticed that whenever he was speaking he was constantly interrupted by a rather large, heavyset woman who told story after story about one experience or another, never running out of tales to tell. She was quite humorous, and when I asked Mom about her later, she told me the woman was Samuel's mother, Loretta. Adding, "She has the same number of children that I have."

I looked across the aisle and saw her sitting in a front pew. Interesting, I thought, that the tall man's mother doesn't seem to have a problem interrupting him. So different from my family—where no one would ever dare interrupt my father. Not his children, not his wives... and very possibly, not even his own mother.

I looked at Samuel again, patiently waiting for his bride to meet him at the altar—then, as the last few seats were filled, I watched as Mama Vee quietly made her way to the piano. As she began playing the *Wedding March,* everyone stood up and faced the French doors at the back of the room. Then the doors slowly opened and in walked Dad with Amy on his arm. She looked so beautiful, like the wedding Barbie dolls I'd seen in a magazine, except she was shorter. Her blonde hair was curled beneath her veil and flowed down over her shoulders. Her eyes sparkled with happiness and her smile was as bright as the sun.

As Mama Vee continued playing the *Wedding March,* Amy and Dad made their way up the aisle and stopped next to Samuel, whose smile was as big and as bright as Amy's. They lovingly looked at each other, then bowed their heads and prepared to pray. The entire congregation bowed their heads as well, then the prayer began. But my eyes were still open because I couldn't stop staring at Amy... She had her eyes closed and as I watched her, I kept thinking about how beautiful her dress had turned out. The white satin bodice with all the pretty beads and lace, along with the train that seemed to go on forever, fit her perfectly. And her veil, made of white lace and more beads, was gorgeous.

This was the first time I had ever been to a wedding, and it stirred something inside me... Someday, I want to be a bride just as beautiful as Amy, I thought. I want to have a big wedding with lots of family and friends. I want to feel special, with people catering to me—just like they catered to her today. I'd even like Dad to escort me to my waiting groom... It would make me so happy to have him be proud of me while I hold onto his arm as he walks me down the aisle like a princess! I know I'm not a real princess, but it would be fun to pretend to be one for a few minutes—all dressed in white with my hair done up and makeup on. Some pretty shoes and maybe even some earrings! Dare I dream? I asked myself... Dare I dream that Dad would join me in my princess-world and pretend I was a jewel to be treasured? Maybe he would—for just one day—if I do what he says and follow all the rules the prophets have taught, then maybe he would.

I'm going to try, I decided—still staring at Amy. I'm going to make Dad proud of me even if I'm just one more child that's been added to the bunch... I'm going to make him proud to be my father, to walk me down the aisle—looking just as proud as he looked when he walked beside Amy.

When the prayer was over, everyone watched quietly as the ceremony proceeded. A few chosen people got up to speak and then Dad, with the authority he possessed as her father, performed the ceremony—giving Amy, in marriage, to Samuel.

After the ceremony there was a dinner held at Mama Louise's house, then everyone returned to the church for the reception. There was dancing and visiting, then came the singing of Mom's special song for Samuel and Amy—the one we had all practiced for so long.

I had memorized every note and every word so well but as I stood with the rest of the family to sing, not a single word would come out... I fought back the tears as a lump began to form in my throat. I clutched my hands together beneath my chin and tried to sing, but I just couldn't. The empty, lonely feeling in my heart overwhelmed me and all I could do was cry.

Silently, I reprimanded myself—demanding to know why I could not sing what I had practiced for weeks and, up until now, could sing perfectly. But it didn't do any good—the tears continued to pour down my face as I pictured myself not seeing Amy at prayer meetings anymore. Not being able to help her do her mom's laundry or help her with the dishes.

The song was over before I knew it, and Amy and Samuel were both smiling from ear to ear. Mom said that the younger kids had to go home after the song was over, so I made my way over to the happy couple to say goodnight and goodbye.

Much taller than me, Amy bent her knees—gracefully floating downward so she could look into my eyes. Whatever she saw there, made her wrap her arms around me and hug me tight. Then placing her hands on my shoulders, she gently pushed me back so she could see my eyes again. As a tear ran down her face, she whispered, "I'll be back to visit, I promise." Then she hugged me again, stood up, and took Samuel's hand.

CHAPTER SIX

WAKING UP AS AN ADULT

In my world, an eleven-year-old adult is not an uncommon thing. What is uncommon, is for the eleven-year-old adult to question why the real adults, who make real decisions, based on real prophecies, cannot seem to cope with the realness of their choices.

For the children of polygamy, childhood can be very short—and mine ended when I was eleven years old. It seems that one night I went to bed as a child, and woke up the next morning as an adult—suddenly responsible for an entire household which consisted of my mother, myself, and my eight siblings—the youngest, just a little more than a year old.

Mom's oldest son has gone to the U.S. to find work, and her two oldest daughters have both married and moved out as well. So I am now the oldest daughter living at home—a daughter whose mother spends her time reading romance novels while I do most of the cooking, cleaning, laundry, and looking after the little ones.

Mom seems to be emotionally distraught and overwhelmed. After all the years of taking care of her own children, with very little help from my father, along with constantly competing for his attention, emotionally supporting his other wives and their children, and keeping up with the expectations of the church, she seems to have crawled into a place of refuge—with a book. Perhaps the words on those pages take her to another world where she is free. Or perhaps they give her something to hope for. I don't know.

Taking care of everyone is a tremendous responsibility, and as hard as it has always been for my mother, it is twice as hard for me—although I love her deeply and I want to do whatever I can to help her. But while she is reading novels the heaps of laundry are getting higher and the dirty dishes are piling up. So, except during school recess, I no longer have time to play like a normal eleven-year-old, and every day when I return home from school there are hours of housework waiting for me.

We finally have electricity and a light socket in each area of the house, along with a few outlets; and we have a Maytag wringer washer and a stone grinder for grinding wheat to make bread. I am so grateful for these things because they make our lives a little easier—although the workload never seems to end. Even with a wringer washer, there are always piles of dirty clothes everywhere I look; and even though there is now a light in the kitchen, the dirty dishes still refuse to wash themselves. And when I have finally conquered the housework, there is always a hungry child, a tired child, a child who needs to be bathed, or a child who needs to be held—and it is up to me to take care of them all.

Just when I thought things would never change, the leader of the Adenites was captured and died in prison, which was wonderful news. At least I no longer had to contend with the fear of being killed by ruthless vigilantes, and although many believed that his followers would continue to pillage and harm, I hoped the leaderless group would eventually disintegrate. Then, unexpectedly, following the death of a monster, Dad suddenly announced that it was time for us to move to Chihuahua.

I was sure the tide had finally turned, and I was so excited about moving… Mom's sister, Aunt Sally, lived in Chihuahua; and just the thought of living near her made my heart sing. She had come to visit us a few times in Baja, and she always showed me so much love—making me feel extra special by always calling me Dolly.

Her oldest daughter was a jewel as well. She also treated me with kindness and love, and she always made me feel as though I was a valuable human being (even though I was just a girl trying my best to survive the pitfalls of being born into a world where a daughter's worth was never acknowledged by men *or* God). So, of course—inwardly desperate to find a reason for my own existence—I looked forward to spending more time with them.

With a spark of renewed energy, Mom began packing up the kitchen—an array of mostly chipped bowls, dented pots and pans, old spoons, glasses and cups. Nothing really worth taking with us—except for the wheat grinder—but it's what we had and very possibly all we might ever have, so it was going with us.

Finishing up in the kitchen while Mom hunted down more boxes, I found a cookie jar without a lid still sitting on one of the shelves. It was full of odds and ends, a couple of matchboxes, and a few folded-up scraps of paper. I needed to use the outhouse, so I grabbed one of the folded papers from the jar and took it with me to the outhouse to use as tissue paper.

I had heard that very few people in Chihuahua still had outhouses, and I was looking forward to saying goodbye to this one. I sat down on the cutout hole, opening up the paper I had taken from the jar, intending to wrinkle it up to make it softer but stopped when I saw Mom's handwriting on it. Although I couldn't read English very well yet, I could read enough to know that this was a note Mom had written to Dad:

> *Your love for Louise is like a cup that is overflowing, leaving nothing to put into my cup. I don't think it is fair.*

I wasn't sure the note had ever been given to Dad, but from what I could gather Mom was letting him know that she was unhappy and tired of getting leftovers. Glancing at it again, I suddenly felt as if I had committed a crime just by reading it—and not wanting Mom to know that I had found it, I quickly folded it up. Anxious to put it back before she noticed it was gone, I yanked up my pants and rushed back to the kitchen, dropping the note into the cookie jar before Mom came back into the room.

This was the first time I realized that my mother had secrets of her own, although I had often wondered why her eyes were red after her long visits with Dad in his parked truck. I thought maybe he was getting after her, like he got after her children—including me—but I never stopped to think that she was unhappy with him or felt that she was being treated unfairly.

It was five o'clock in the morning and still dark outside when I heard Mom's voice ringing through the sheet-walls. "Get up kids, Dad is going to be here in a few minutes!" she said briskly. "He's expecting us to be ready to leave. Vera, help me get these kids some mush!"

Rubbing my eyes, I stumbled out of bed. I was less than half-awake, and my body felt exhausted from the day before. From early in the morning until I went to bed, I had helped Mom sort and pack. We were taking all the clothes and almost everything in the kitchen; the rest we were leaving behind.

After helping feed the kids, then washing their faces and combing their hair, I decided to take a quick walk through the house knowing that I'd never be seeing it again. All the lights were on as I walked through the sheet-walls expecting to feel sad about leaving and thoroughly surprised when I didn't. Instead, I felt a wave of excitement wash over me.

I peeked into the bathroom from the common area... The shelves, made of old boards, lined half the room. A white tub with no faucet sat in the corner, reminding me of Mom's dream to make the tub functional someday. And, of course, there was no toilet—but the old, faithful pot sat empty between the tub and more shelves.

Next, I poked my head through the sheeted walls of one of the bedrooms—but there wasn't much to look at, just bed frames made of old boards with mattresses thrown on top. Old, stinky mattresses! Mom had a lot of bed wetter's and the mattresses were stained and smelled horrible. Just looking at them made me remember the many nights I had woken up to find myself soaked from head to toe from one sibling or another wetting the bed; hating when it got in my hair!

I quietly walked into Mom's room. After many years of dingy sheets hanging from the ceiling, she had finally divided her room off from the rest with a framed wall made of plywood. I'm sure she wanted some privacy with Dad when it was her turn to have a night with him but, sadly, I could not recall a single time when Dad woke up at our house. If he had ever spent the night here, I was not aware of it.

I took a moment and sat down on the raggedy couch in the front room. A very worn-out throw rug was on the floor in front of it. Staring at the rug, I recalled the many evenings we sat around Mom on the couch, or on the floor, as she played her guitar or her accordion and sang with us. She had an old record player someone had given her that she treasured—and when Aunt Sally came to visit us, she brought Mom records by Kenny Rogers, Willie Nelson, Patsy Cline and a few others which she played over and over... Mom loved music, and right here in this front room is where she taught us to love and appreciate music too. She also spent a lot of evenings reading books to us. Story time with her in this room was the best! We might not have received much love from Dad—he only filled us with the Gospel and the fear of hell—but we all received plenty of love from Mom. She wasn't very expressive with words about her love for us, but she taught us to value and love others through kindness. And, although I don't remember her ever saying the words, "I love you," I always knew that she did.

Getting up from the couch, I went into the kitchen... So many meals were prepared and shared in this room—occasionally with Dad, but most of the time just with Mom. Again, fond memories flooded my mind. All the big batches of bread Mom made, and the countless pots of beans and potatoes—all made and served with love. Memories of the times we sat around the table telling stories, and the times I would get up early in the morning and find Mom sitting with a friend—sharing a cup of coffee and the scriptures, studying the gospel together... And dishes! I will never forget the mountains of dishes I washed in this kitchen, and the green-painted cement floor with all the holes in it that I swept every day. Nor will I forget the times we sat around the table waiting for the scones Mom made by frying bread dough and sprinkling sugar on top, or all the canning and preserving that took place in this kitchen when Dad would get permission from the farmers who lived a few hours away to come in and pick through the leftovers in their fields when they were done harvesting. Tomatoes, potatoes, quince and, occasionally, grapes... Dad would take all of us—and tons of brown gunnysacks, tubs and pails—and send us out into the fields to pick what was left after the harvest. When we were finished, everything would be divided up amongst Dad's wives and we would all get busy canning. It seemed that the other wives had jars of the stuff all year because they had strict rules about how often their kids could eat it. But not at our house! Mom would let us have it constantly until it was gone, which was usually only a few weeks... So many memories in this kitchen. So much love. So much sharing.

Suddenly hearing a truck pull up in the front yard, I let my thoughts return to the present moment. It was Dad driving a white and blue one-ton truck. The back was all camper with an area above the cab where there was a mattress to sleep on, and windows in the front and side.

Jumping out of the driver's seat, Dad's familiar whistle—the whistle he used whenever he wanted to get the whole family's attention—sliced through the air. It was not a whistle any of us ever ignored, and I knew I'd better hurry and help get all the kids into the truck.

It was still dark, but the headlights lit the front of the house and the surrounding area enough for us to see. "Load up!" Dad ordered, as we all jumped into the back of the truck.

I climbed up into the area above the cab just in time to see the lights in our old house go off and Mom's shadowy figure walk around the truck to the passenger side. The truck door slammed shut, then I heard it open again. A few seconds later, the side door to the back of the truck opened, and Mom said softly, "You kids stay away from the door, okay? Vera, keep an eye on them for me." When she was back in the passenger seat, Dad eased the big truck past the old, scary tree in the front yard, and we were on our way.

Passing Mama Nadine's house, I remembered Mom telling me that Dad would be coming back for each of his other wives after taking us to Chihuahua. We were the first to go because Mom's family was having a reunion at Aunt Sally's house and she didn't want to miss the family gathering. So, for once, Dad put us first—and I hoped with all my heart that Mom was smiling.

CHAPTER SEVEN

THE ROAD TO PARADISE

It's not that all good things come to an end—it's that Life is a two-way street, and the road that takes you to Paradise is the same road that takes you back to wherever you came from... All you've got to do is make one U-turn.

The trip from Baja to Chihuahua was long and grueling. After two days of being cooped up in the back of the stifling truck with the other kids, I wanted to jump for joy when Dad finally announced that we were only a few hours away from Chihuahua. One at a time, the other kids had taken turns sitting in the front with Mom and Dad, but I had not. I was too afraid that one of my brothers or sisters might open the door and fall out if I wasn't there to keep my eye on them, so I remained in the back—praying that our new home was just around the next bend.

The weather was noticeably different in this part of Mexico—hot and dry, instead of humid and breezy like Baja. As we got closer to our destination, I could see a hill with a huge, white "S" on it—standing for "Saunders" and created with painted boulders.

We were definitely in Chihuahua, and our new home was in a valley nestled at the foot of the hill with a few other hills surrounding it. The town was named after the prophet, A.D. Saunders, and is often referred to as "Saunders" or simply, "the colony." I was told that it started out as a ranch that A.D. Saunders and his sons had purchased long ago, then later became what is now known as Colonia Saunders. I could see some homes and orchards as we made our way down into the valley, then Dad suddenly slowed down, exiting the main highway and turning onto a dirt road.

We're finally here, I thought... This is the place where it all started. This is the place God asked his people to live to escape the final-day calamities in the U.S. This is the promised land. Suddenly, I felt confused... Why had Dad moved his family to Baja if God had planned to establish His kingdom here? It didn't make any sense to me, but I decided it didn't matter. We're here now, I told myself, and in a few minutes we'll be at our new home in Saunders—the promised land—where we will be part of a community doing God's work.

I felt excited as we pulled up next to a cute cement house with rosebushes and hedges planted in the front next to patches of green grass. A sidewalk led to the front door. Dad and Mom hopped out of the truck, taking the walkway to the front door. I watched from the side windows above the cab to see who came out to greet them... Amy! It was Amy!

Mom and Dad had decided to stop at her house and say hello before going to my older sister's new home. I quickly jumped out of the truck and ran up to her, almost knocking her over with my hug. She had a little boy now, Andrew, whom she was holding in her arms and proudly showing off to us. Dad was curious to know where her husband was, and Amy told him that Samuel was out irrigating a field and would not be home for a while. It had been a long trip, and Mom seemed a little anxious to get going, so we hugged goodbye, got back in the truck, and continued to my sister's house.

Only a few blocks away, we arrived within minutes. My older sister, Cheryl, had married Samuel's younger brother. She was his second wife and was living in the same home with him and his first wife, Rhonda. Their home was very small but cute as can be. Each wife had their own bedroom and bathroom but shared the same kitchen and living room. It was so much nicer than our home in Baja.

Cheryl and Rhonda received us with open arms. They prepared a delicious meal for us, then made sure we had plenty of clean towels to use after taking baths. It felt wonderful to be received with so much love and to be treated so well. Feeling fresh and clean again, I fell asleep thinking about Mom's family reunion, which would be taking place tomorrow at Aunt Sally's house.

It was wonderful seeing all of Mom's family together in one place. Even Grandma had come all the way from the U.S. to join us! The whole day was a happy event, but the very best part of it came last…

Toward the end of the reunion, I overheard Mom say that Grandma had invited us to come to the U.S. to live—and that she planned to take all her children to Odessa, Texas so she could be closer to her own mother for a while.

Stay with Grandma? Wow, I thought, life just keeps getting better and better. I can't wait to get to Texas!

Whenever Grandma came to visit us in Baja, she always brought lots of toys and food from the United States. Mom said Grandma was a hard worker and that she'd made a lot of money fixing up and selling houses. She owned a lot of property now, and Mom told us that she loved sharing her wealth with her family and with people in need.

Grandma had long, white hair that she twisted into a French bun and fastened with lots of bobby pins. She wore beautiful silk blouses tucked into her nice dress slacks, and a splash of perfume, and bright lipstick—with pretty earrings and rings on her fingers. From her head right down to her perfectly manicured toenails—which peeked out from her fashionable sandals—Grandma always looked beautiful. But the most beautiful part of her was her smile, which was always filled with love and adoration... On her visits to Baja, she often thanked me for helping Mom out so much and made sure to bring me little extra-special gifts, like pretty barrettes or a new brush. I always looked forward to her coming to visit us, and I absolutely loved the idea of going to stay with her for a while.

A few days after Grandma left Chihuahua to return home, Dad's new wife, Susan, came to pick us up at Aunt Sally's. She was going to be taking us across the border to the United States, then on to Grandma's house in Odessa, Texas.

I didn't know Susan at all. She had been married to Samuels's dad, Victor—and after he was killed in a car accident, Dad married Susan along with one of Victor's other wives, Karen. (In our religion, widows were to be taken care of by the other men in the church. So it was never long after a man died that other men in the congregation would marry the wives he left behind—and, in this case, Dad married two of Victor's six wives.)

Susan seemed very nice as I listened to her and Mom talking with each other during the trip. We rode for eight hours in her cargo van, which had plenty of space. She had thrown a few blankets in the back along with some pillows for us to lay on, and it wasn't long before we were all sleeping.

It was dark when I woke up. The van had stopped, and we were parked in a driveway. This must be Grandma's house, I thought, squinting my eyes but not able to see much of anything in the dark. The feeling in the air was different from anything I had ever felt before. It felt like hope and ease... Suddenly, the front porch lit up. Blinking, I saw Mom and Susan coming back to the van and Grandma waiting for us at the door wearing a white robe and a pair of blue slippers.

Mom opened the back of the van, and as I waited for my brothers and sisters to jump out, I felt a tidal wave of excitement surging through me. I could hardly wait to wrap my arms around Grandma and as soon as I reached her, I hugged her tight. As usual, she felt and smelled wonderful.

It was the middle of the night, and after visiting for a few minutes, Grandma led me to the room I would be staying in. It had two twin beds with light blue covers. The walls were adorned with beautiful artwork, and the carpet beneath my feet felt thick and soft. Grandma pulled down the cover on one of the beds, revealing the pretty, flowered sheets. "You can sleep in this bed," she said. "Your brothers will be staying in the room across the hall and your mother will be in the room at the end of the hall, along with your baby sisters." She smiled, "And the bathroom is next to the boys' room," she added.

A bed all to myself, I thought, with clean sheets and blankets? This was something I had always dreamed of!

Grandma waited for me to hop into bed. I quickly hugged her again, then thanked her. She smiled her usual loving smile then turned the lights off and quietly left the room.

As I lay there with the nightlight casting a soft glow around the room, I was in total awe of my surroundings. I felt blessed. So blessed... I closed my eyes and silently said a different kind of prayer—not a prayer I usually said—not a begging and pleading for forgiveness prayer, or a request for a few more comforts prayer.... This time, I felt different as I prayed:

> *Dear Heavenly Father, thank you for letting us come to the United States even though the prophets have told us not to come here. They have said that it is a wicked place with mostly wicked people that you are going to destroy for not living your laws. But Grandma lives here, and I know she's not wicked, God. Thank you for watching over*

her. I wish you would let us live here too. It feels so right to be here. I understand what Dad has said about you needing us to do your work in Mexico, but I just wish we didn't have to live down there anymore. Can't we do your work here? If there is any way you can let us live here, God, please do. This I pray in the name of your son, Jesus Christ. Amen.

I soon fell asleep, but when I opened my eyes the next morning, I was confused. Everything looked different, and I wasn't sure where I was... The room was clean and bright, and it had real walls that were painted white. The sun was shining through the sheer curtains that covered the windows. I looked down at the carpeted floor and suddenly remembered where I was... In the United States at Grandma's house!

A wonderful aroma was coming from somewhere. It smelled like waffles, which I only had on special occasions when I stayed at Mama Vee's house. (She was the only one in the family with a waffle iron and real syrup.)

My first instinct was to jump out of bed and run to the kitchen before all the waffles were gone, then I remembered that I was at Grandma's house and there really was no need to hurry. Of course there would be plenty for everyone, and I didn't need to worry about going without. So, instead of rushing, I relaxed back into the fluffy pillows and the soft cotton sheets, pulling them up over my head as I stretched and basked in the comfort and luxury of the bed—taking time to enjoy this little piece of Paradise.

The bathroom was beautiful... A bathtub and a sink with running water—warm water—along with a toilet that you actually flushed. Everything felt so fresh and clean. Grandma had laid out new toothbrushes and toothpaste for us, but I had to go and get Mom to show me how to use them. Even though I was eleven years old, I had never brushed my teeth before... I'd watched Mom do it at home in

Baja a few times, but I always thought it was something special that only grown-ups got to do. So, my first experience with a toothbrush was incredible! I loved how clean teeth felt and for the rest of the day I kept rubbing my tongue over them. I couldn't get over how smooth they felt, and I was so excited when Grandma told me I could keep the toothbrush and toothpaste I had used!

After taking a warm bath and getting dressed in my brother's clothes again, I found my way to the kitchen. There was a lot of noise coming from the front room, so I poked my head through the doorway and could see my siblings sprawled out on the floor with their eyes glued to the television. They were watching Bugs Bunny cartoons. And they were loving every minute of it!

Mom and Grandma were sitting at the kitchen table talking while drinking their coffee and eating waffles. There was syrup, strawberry jam, butter, milk, and a mountain of waffles heaped on a plate in the center of the table. "Good morning," said Grandma, smiling at me. "How did you sleep?"

"Good," I answered, not wanting to sound overly excited about something as simple (and as wonderful) as a good night's sleep.

"Help yourself to some breakfast," she said, handing me a plate and a glass for milk. Then, pointing to a basket filled with apples, bananas, and oranges, she added, "There's some fruit there, too, if you'd like."

Mom and Grandma continued with their conversation as I helped myself to breakfast, which felt like a feast... Just how I imagined a princess might dine at a palace!

I listened as Grandma described an apartment she wanted Mom to look at. It was located in a complex that Grandma owned, and it was right next to Mom's sister, Carla, and her brother.

Why would Grandma want Mom to look at an apartment, I wondered—does she want us to live here permanently? Could it be possible that she does? I hope it's so, I thought, as I secretly absorbed every word Grandma was saying to Mom:

"Maybe you just need some time away to clear your mind," Grandma said.

"I do love him," said Mom quietly, "but it's just so hard."

I suddenly remembered the letter I'd found in the cookie jar in Baja and wondered if perhaps Mom had given that letter to Dad... Maybe we came to Texas because Mom wasn't happy living with him in Mexico anymore and she wanted us to live in the U.S. forever... A burst of inner-happiness almost gave me away. I wanted to jump up and down with joy but not wanting Mom to know that I was listening to her private conversation, I sat still and pretended I was watching cartoons as I finished eating my breakfast.

Later that day, Mom came into the living room where I was watching television with the kids and announced that she and Grandma were going to look at an apartment for us to live in. "Keep an eye on the kids, Vera," she said, slipping out of the room before I could ask her any questions.

She thinks I don't know that something is up between her and Dad, I thought. And I'm going to keep it that way. I'm afraid that if she talks about it, she might change her mind and we'll have to go back to Mexico. I'm going to enjoy my new life in the States and try not to think about Dad's prophets and their warnings about living here.

Our new apartment was wonderful. It had a full bathroom, a kitchen with appliances, and closets to hang our clothes. We had a television in our front room and lots of food in the cupboards. Grandma took me shopping and bought me new shoes and clothes, along with underwear that fit me. No more wearing my brother's clothes... She even bought me a purse!

My new school was just as wonderful as my new home. It had bright and spacious classrooms that were organized and clean. Lunch hours with warm meals and chocolate milk. Music and art classes, too! I loved it here!

I still had to take care of most of the housework and my siblings, but I didn't mind. It wasn't as hard as it was in Mexico, and besides, it seemed like Mom was doing more to help. Whenever we went to Grandma's house to visit, I felt a strong desire to find ways to give back to her all she was doing for us. I would clean different rooms from top to bottom, making everything sparkle. But whenever Grandma would catch me, she would say things like, "You don't have to do that, Vera." Or, "Go have fun with the kids."

On one occasion I overheard her getting after Mom. "She's just a child, Patrice. You shouldn't be having her do so much of the work." And, although I felt special because Grandma was concerned about how much I was doing, I didn't really want to quit helping Mom. It was the only way I knew how to show her that I loved her, and it was my way of showing my siblings that I loved them too.

My life in America was amazing, and I hoped it would never end—but it did. It was a beautiful, sunny morning. I was in English class when I heard an announcement over the loudspeaker: "Vera Jackson, please report to the principal's office."

I gasped when I heard my name, wondering what in the world I had done to get myself in trouble. I asked to be excused from class and quickly made my way down the long hall leading to the principal's office. I walked through the door and was surprised to see Mom sitting in one of the chairs. My stomach flipped when I realized that I must be in major trouble for her to have been called in. But she smiled at me, then said something I never expected to hear her say, "I'm here to pick you up because we are going back to Mexico."

What? NO! I love our new life here! This can't be happening, I thought. But before I could ask her why, she instructed me to get my things and to meet her in the school parking lot—then added that she would be waiting for me, along with my siblings… I did as

I was told but kept wondering why we were leaving so suddenly. Mom had never actually told me why we had moved here, and I was sure she wasn't planning on telling me why we were moving back. But I needed to find a way to ask her…

I walked out the school doors and down the sidewalk to the parking lot where Mom was busy loading my brothers and sisters into a vehicle. I stopped and watched for a few minutes, wondering how I could go about asking her why we were leaving. I knew I didn't have a right to question her decisions. After all, I was a kid and I should know better than to question a parent.

Mom turned around and saw me standing there. "Come on, Vera, let's go," she said. "What are you waiting for?"

I walked over to the car and slid into the passenger seat. After closing the door, I turned to look at Mom. I decided that now was just as good a time as any to ask her my question, so I blurted it out, "Mom, why are we leaving?"

I expected her to explain what was going on between her and Dad, and I expected her to say that things were all better between them now, but she said something totally unexpected. "This isn't a good place for us to live, Vera. The school has been trying to force me to give you kids immunization shots and you know it's against our religion. The government is trying to control everyone out here so they can have power over us. This is exactly what the prophet said was going to happen before the destruction of the United States begins. Your Dad called me and talked to me about this yesterday— and he is right. It's time for us to go back."

I couldn't quite understand Mom's reasoning. Many of our family members lived in the States and they were fine. And, because of the letter I'd found, in my heart I truly believed that Mom wanted a different life. But the power my dad had over her mind, along with her desire to do what was right to make it to the celestial glory, must have been far greater than her own personal needs.

So, back to Mexico it was. Our cousin, Mark, drove us back. Mom had collected a lot of new things during our six-month stay in Odessa, and Grandma had been quite generous, so Mark's truck was packed full—leaving just enough room in the back for the kids. Sadly, I didn't get to say goodbye to Grandma. We left in the middle of the day while she was still at work but, in my heart, I thanked her for all she had done for us.

As fun as being a businesswoman like Grandma seemed, I quickly decided I dare not dream such elaborate dreams. Living God's laws should be most important to me and doing what Grandma does wasn't part of the laws I had been taught. Living celestial marriage is my destiny, I told myself—but somewhere deep in my soul I could sense a presence that was shaking its head saying, "No. No it's not!" Then suddenly an image of God, one that seemed to be a reflection of Dad, shook his head, saying, "Yes. Yes it is!"

I did not yet trust the voice that was saying "no," so I stuck with what felt familiar... Dad, and the God I have learned about from him, is who I need to listen to, I decided.

And so I did.

CHAPTER EIGHT

FLEETING FIRST LOVE

Love is magic. It transforms ordinary pieces of time into extraordinary moments—moments that cling to your heart and remain there forever.

At first, being back in Mexico was like drinking a potion made of laughter and tears… Although I felt sad because we were no longer in Texas, I felt happier about being in Saunders than in Baja. There were significantly more members of Jerome's church living here and it seemed that most of them were thriving. The quality of everyday life was far above the debilitating poverty we had endured in Baja. Here, the living conditions and houses were much nicer, and most had indoor plumbing, electricity, and real walls.

While we were in the U.S., Dad had moved the rest of his wives and children to this community. He couldn't purchase homes for them yet, but he managed to borrow enough empty houses throughout the town for his many wives and children to live in. Some homeowners were moving back to the States after losing faith in the church, leaving their empty houses behind. Others were buying surrounding land and planting orchards for future benefit, which inevitably took them to the States where they worked tirelessly to finance their future-lives in Saunders—leaving plenty of vacant homes for Dad to borrow.

When our prophet, Jerome, was killed, many church members had wrestled with what to do next. Some members—including my dad—were waiting patiently for God to send a new prophet which they believed could happen any day. Others stayed in Mexico but made a life out of going back and forth to the States. These men selectively chose what parts of the gospel were convenient for them to keep living. Plural marriage was convenient. Staying out of the United States was not. Then there were those who gave up on all Jerome's teachings—except for polygamy. They used this law as a license to cheat on their wives, in the name of God—which apparently made it all right. Our women, however, were still subject to God's laws and to their husbands. But the men without a prophet to answer to, seemed to care only about themselves and their rampant, selfish desires.

Fighting began amongst the men. For the most part, they argued about who held more authority (due to being ordained by Jerome, the prophet) as an apostle or a patriarch. The town began to divide into groups, each believing they held authority or that they would be the next in line to receive the priesthood. But, although all this bickering was taking place, the fundamental beliefs remained the same amongst each group. Celestial marriage was the only way to enter the Kingdom of Heaven and was taught and practiced by each group. All social events were enjoyed together, regardless of the group you belonged to. The ongoing theme among all of them was the same: Men were more valued by God than women; and women needed men to make it to Heaven. Dad explained it to me countless times, saying, "If God's kingdom were established on Earth today, the women would open doors for the men, and the women would lay their petticoats down in the mud puddles for the men—instead of the other way around." And, of course, I believed him.

The home Dad borrowed for us to live in was L-shaped and had three bedrooms, a large bathroom, a kitchen with a built-in table and lots of cabinets made of smooth, glossy wood, a dining room, and living room. It also had hot and cold running water, beautiful tiled floors, and walks leading to the front door from the driveway.

Our borrowed home belonged to the only midwife in town. She had a degree in nursing and her husband was a well-educated engineer. They were converted to the church in the early stages and had moved here from the U.S. but had decided to return for a short time and allowed us to stay in their home while they were away. It was while living in this home that I experienced what I thought Mom might be reading about in all those romance novels... Love. Sweet Love. Love that you never forget.

It was my first day at the local public school, which was located on the other side of the main highway running through town. I wore a new outfit I had gotten in Texas, and I had the pretty purse Grandma had bought for me—both, lifting my spirits and giving me a just-recently-found confidence in my appearance.

I was sitting at my assigned desk next to Bonita when the cutest boy I had ever seen walked into the room. He was my height and, like me, he had blonde hair and green eyes. Out of the corner of my eye, I saw him glance my way as he passed my desk, taking a seat behind me, but a little off to the side. Turning slightly, I nervously smiled at him and he smiled back. The teacher pulled out the roll-call list and began calling out names.

"Vera Jackson?" he called out.

I raised my hand and answered, "Present."

"Gregario Sheridan?" he said, looking up from his list.

I watched as the cute boy raised his hand and said, "Present."

Gregario Sheridan, I mused... I want to get to know you.

When the bell rang for recess, I followed my classmates out the door—heading toward a woman standing on the other side of the school fence with a box of treats. The kids stood inside the fence, asking for what they wanted, while she poked her hand through the chain-link fence, exchanging goodies for pesos.

As I stood there watching everyone buying chips and candy, my friend, Kristen, walked up to me along with Gregario and another boy. "Vera," she said, "this is Gregario and Neal."

I smiled. "Hi, I'm Vera," I said, secretly swooning. "It's nice to meet you."

"I know who you are," Gregario said. "You're one of the Jackson girls. My dad likes your dad a lot."

When the group of kids buying treats disappeared, Gregario walked up to the lady and asked her for something in Spanish, then he turned around and asked me if I wanted some churros with chili.

"Sure," I said, feeling slightly embarrassed but flattered at the same time.

Gregario paid for our food and handed me my churros, then we walked toward the basketball court together. As we stood there laughing and talking and eating, something special blossomed between us.

After that first day, I could not wait to get to school so I could see him. He made me feel so special and every day we spent as much time together as we could. We liked each other a lot. It was undeniable. But that school year ended, and the following year Mom made me go to the private school our community had just opened. It wasn't registered with the state, so the parents who wanted their children to receive diplomas and a state recognized education did not allow their children to go—and both Kristen and Gregario's parents were among them. Because of it, I didn't get to see Gregario every day anymore, which made me terribly sad.

I did get to see Kristen, though—every day after school—and she delivered Gregario's love letters to me, and mine to him. And, oh, how I looked forward to getting those letters! They made only seeing each other occasionally at social events—such as church parties and Friday night square dances—a little easier on my heart.

The few times Gregario and I were together were wonderful... We never ran out of things to talk about and he made me feel as if I was the most special girl in the world. I didn't dare tell Mom how much I loved him. He wasn't a polygamist yet. He was still too young, and I was afraid she would assume he wasn't going to live celestial marriage and that she'd make me stay away from him.

One person I could confide in though, was Amy. She liked him a lot and thought he was nice. Many times, when I went to her house to visit, she would curl my hair and do whatever she could to help me look pretty for him. One day, I asked if I could borrow a pair of her shorts. I was going on a picnic and Gregario was going to be there. She gave me a sad look and, after searching through her drawers for a pair of shorts I could wear, we sat down on her bed and talked.

"You look sad today," I said.

"I am," she answered. "Ever since Samuel married his second wife, Stella, and moved her into my house, things have been kind of hard. I've been good to her, Vera. Honestly, I have. I let her move in with me and take over my daughter's room, but it seems that for one reason or another she's always mad. Samuel is building a new house for her down the road, and I can't wait until it's finished and she moves out. I didn't think living celestial marriage would be this hard... Samuel is doing the best he can, and I love him more than ever, but it's just not as easy as I would like it to be. If Stella would stop getting mad all the time my life would be so much better."

My heart went out to her as I tried to understand what she was going through, but thoughts of Gregario and how I felt when I was around him quickly pulled me back into my own world. So, our conversation drifted back to pink shorts, a white blouse, and how to curl my hair.

As time went by, I noticed that Dad was spending a lot of time with Floyd Saunders, our prophet's brother. Floyd believed he held some type of authority. He didn't claim to be a prophet but the next closest thing—he claimed to be a messenger of God. A messenger who was preparing the way for God's kingdom here on Earth. He settled in Quintana-Roo, a southern state in Mexico, taking a handful of followers along with him. And, for the last few years, he had been trying to convince Dad of his claim and Dad had finally bought into it… He decided that we would be leaving as soon as the last day of school was over and, before I knew it, the school year ended.

Once again, Mom would be the first of Dad's wives to make the three-day trip to yet another new home. And, as we had done before, we packed our belongings in the back of Dad's truck and prepared for the long journey.

I did not want to leave Gregario, but I knew there was nothing I could do about it. I had no say in the matter, so I carefully wrote him a goodbye note and asked Kristen to give it to him.

As sad as it was to be leaving, writing that note gave me a sense of peace because it wasn't a goodbye-forever note, it was only a goodbye-for-now note… I truly believed that when we were a few years older, we would be together again and get married.

A few more years, I thought to myself, as I was leaving our home behind. Just a few more years.

CHAPTER NINE

THE OTHER HELL

I don't think most people realize that there are two levels of hell. The higher-hell is called Baja, Mexico. The lower one, Quintana-roo—a mere two thousand miles between the hell that hath no comforts and the hell that hath no mercy.

The morning of our departure, all the family gathered together at Mama Louise's house to pray. Dad offered the prayer. He asked God to bless him on his endeavor with Floyd and to keep us safe on our trip.

I hugged the family goodbye and didn't allow myself to feel sad. I knew they would all be joining us in the southern tip of Mexico soon. Amy came to see us off just before we started to load the truck and I quickly hugged her goodbye.

"Let's go!" Dad shouted, as we all squeezed into the back of the truck and onto Mom's neatly packed belongings. I chose the spot closest to the window, then laid on my stomach with my arm supporting my head and closed my eyes. I let my thoughts wander to Gregario, silently praying that he knew how much I loved him. Then I began to wonder about the new town we were headed to and hoped it would be as nice as Chihuahua.

We had been on the road for three days. Again, Dad parked the truck on the side of the road so we could eat and find somewhere in the bushes to do our business. As soon as the truck stopped moving, and the wind was no longer blowing through the window, I thought I was going to die. The humidity, along with the blistering heat, made everything feel sticky. I couldn't wait for Dad to let us out of the camper, thinking that I would find some relief outside. But as soon as I got out, I was sure I was going to faint—the damp air was so hot and so heavy that I felt like I was suffocating.

Wild-eyed, I looked at Mom. "It feels like I'm in an oven with steam in it. Why does it feel like this?" I asked.

"It's the normal weather down here," she explained. "It is very humid compared to other parts of Mexico."

Holy cow, this is horrible, I thought. I don't like this place!

I walked toward the greenery on the side of the road in search of a private place to pee. Then I heard Mom holler, "Be careful, Vera, watch out for snakes!"

Snakes? Horrified, I flew back to the truck. I was petrified of snakes! Ever since a rattlesnake brushed up against my leg while I was doing the wash in Chihuahua, I've been terrified of them. After I'd felt it on my leg, I saw it coil itself into a striking position. Luckily, an inner-force helped me take the quickest leap of my life—then a high-speed dash I didn't even know I was capable of. I ran all the way around the house and through the front door at lightning speed. As I stopped to catch my breath, adrenaline still rushing through me, I realized the danger I had just escaped.

In Chihuahua, people usually died when bitten by rattlesnakes. We didn't see them very often but when we did, we had to be extremely careful—they scared me more than God, Dad and the devil put together! There was no way I was going into the bushes to pee, and I quickly decided I would wait until we got to the new town—even if we were still two hours away.

Back on the road again, the wind whipped through the camper windows giving me some relief from the smothering heat, but not for long. As we got closer to our destination, small towns began popping up everywhere—towns full of speed bumps, which made Dad slow down. With no wind blowing through the camper window, the heat was unbearable again. Not only was I dripping with sweat, I swear I was dripping pee, too—and the speed bumps were not helping at all!

All the people in the towns looked the same. They were short with dark skin and big bellies; and the road appeared to be there for them and not cars. They did not move out of the way and paid no attention to the vehicles driving by. They just continued to walk slowly, with big bowls on top of their heads or sacks on their backs, as though we were the intruders of their roadway. It was a wonder Dad didn't accidentally hit one of them! There were tiny houses everywhere—houses made of sticks, woven together with wire or vines, and roofs made from what looked like palm leaves. And, to my surprise, children played outside, either stark naked or in their underwear.

Every so often we would drive through slightly bigger towns, but the people looked the same. Dad told us they were Mayan Indians and were the true Nephites the *Book of Mormon* talked about—and that we were to live amongst the true Nephites, according to Floyd's beliefs.

The bigger towns had grocery stores, small gas stations and restaurants on the sides of the main highway. There were women and children at every speed bump selling fresh fruit, juice, coconut and candy. They seemed desperate for us to buy from them as they practically invaded our vehicle. I noticed that a lot of them had gold in and around their front teeth. I also noticed how they stared at us through the windows of our truck, as if they had never seen people with white skin before. And maybe they hadn't, but I'd never seen people like them before either!

Just as I thought all the little jungle-towns would never end, Dad pulled off the narrow highway. Then he turned onto an even narrower dirt road. I was sure we'd be arriving at our new home any minute, but it took another forty-five minutes before we got a glimpse of our new hometown in Quintana-roo, Mexico. The roads had been bumpy and full of rocks, and I thought for sure my bladder was permanently damaged!

The decrepit little town seemed to be nothing more than a clearing in the middle of a jungle… We drove past two homes that were made of cinderblock, and each had a stick-house with a leaf roof to the side. A big, cement basketball court was in the center of the clearing—encircled with another dirt road. To the side of the road were twelve lots separated by rock fences with homes on each side of them. Some homes were cinderblock, some were stick homes, and some were a combination of both.

After parking in front of one that was a combination of both, Dad turned the truck off. As I got out, I noticed Katrina, an old friend of mine from Chihuahua, walking into the stick house. I assumed it was their chicken coop, but when I went inside and saw a stove, I realized I was wrong. My curiosity was piqued but my need to find a bathroom was all I could think about.

"Katrina!" I yelled, spotting her just before she was about to leave through another opening in the back.

She turned around and smiled at me, then walked back to where I was standing. We hugged each other briefly, then—in an urgent voice—I asked her where the bathroom was.

"Follow me," she said, leading me through the house and out the back.

We walked past the cinderblock house and a tin structure with a door and no roof, down a narrow trail, then up to an even smaller structure made from a few boards with flimsy tin walls. She opened the door, exposing something I was already very familiar with. A stinky outhouse! But this one was much worse than our outhouse in Baja.

When I stepped inside, Katrina let the door go. It quickly slammed shut, thanks to hinges made of old, cut-up tires. "I'll wait right here for you," I heard her say as I struggled to get my pants down in time. I sat down over the cutout opening and peed for what felt like an hour. While I sat there, I couldn't help but notice all the rusty holes in the tin that left me without much privacy.

I might as well be peeing in public, I thought. Then I looked down into the hole I was sitting on and noticed that it was very shallow, probably because there were too many big rocks to allow it to be dug any deeper. I felt utterly disgusted as I watched the flies having a field day. Their buzzing was so loud I could hardly hear myself think. Back to this again, I muttered to myself, as I drip dried and pulled my pants up.

Physically, I felt much better now that I had used the outhouse, but I had a terrible sinking feeling inside my heart. I'd been looking forward to our new life being more like it had been in Chihuahua, but from the looks of things it was going to be even worse than in Baja.

As we followed the trail back, Katrina explained how most people survived this unconventional way of life—as if it were nothing unusual! We stopped at the first tin structure we had passed on our way to the outhouse. She opened the door and asked me if I wanted to look inside. I peered into an eight-by-eight room made the same way the outhouse was. It, too, was full of big, ragged holes. I stepped inside and the first thing I noticed was an old, rusty cake pan—which looked like it had been punctured with something sharp to make little holes—nailed to a supporting board that ran across the roofless structure. A poor man's showerhead, I thought, noticing the black water hose running from the floor all the way up into the cake pan. The floor was made of rough cement, and a very-visible four-inch PVC drainpipe diverted the water outside. A grungy bar of soap and a cheap bottle of Mexican shampoo sat on a slab of wood in a corner. On the inside of the door, near the top, was a board with a few large nails protruding from it—used, I assumed, for hanging clothes or towels.

"This is the grand, elaborate shower room," Katrina said, trying to be humorous, although I found nothing funny about showering out in the open!

Leaving the shower room, I followed her to the cinderblock house adjacent to the stick house. When we stepped inside, I thought I would melt from the heat. The house had a small screened-in porch and two tiny rooms—each, just big enough for one bed surrounded by nets hanging from the ceiling.

"What are those for?" I asked, staring at the nets.

"To keep mosquitoes from biting us while we sleep," she answered. "Mosquitoes are really bad here and a lot of them carry malaria and dysentery. The government tries to get rid of them by putting out poison, but we still have to take precautions. There is also a type of fly called 'Tabano.' When it stings you, it can lay an egg in you that later hatches as a worm."

My stomach turned, I began to feel sick as she went on, "We also have to take worm medicine every four months here. Most of the Mayans just let their pigs roam the streets leaving their feces wherever they go—and it constantly exposes us to getting worms."

Katrina had lived in Chihuahua when I lived there but had moved here when her mother married Floyd, right after her dad died. She seemed totally accepting of this muggy, bug-infested, poverty-stricken place and I hoped I would eventually be as strong as she was.

She finished showing me what she called the *sleep house,* then said, "Come on, I'll show you the kitchen."

It was now dark outside. "Wait while I grab a flashlight," she added, then ran into one of the bedrooms, quickly returning with a red flashlight. "We don't go anywhere at night without one of these," she explained, turning it on. "We each have our own, and at night I use mine everywhere I go—even if I'm only taking the short pathway to the kitchen—because I never know when I might run into a snake."

Oh God, I thought, as she proceeded to tell me that the two most poisonous snakes in this part of Mexico were the Coral Snake and the Cuatro Nariz. "I've seen lots of them since we moved here," she said calmly. "I've even had to kill a few with a machete. You do know what a machete is, right?"

"No," I said, wondering if I was supposed to know.

"A machete is a vital tool down here that no one lives without. Not only do we use it to keep the fast-growing brush down, but it also helps keep us safe."

"Safe from what?" I asked.

"Safe from snakes, scorpions and tarantulas that love to come visit us inside our homes," she replied.

As she continued talking, I began feeling worse. It was getting harder for me to breathe; and not only was the heat and humidity suffocating me, but panic was beginning to set in. I stayed as close to her and the flashlight as possible, clutching my stomach as I followed her to the kitchen. She opened the splintered, rotting door by reaching her hand over the top of it and unhooking the latch—which was made from two bent nails. Inside, her sister, Janice, was swinging in a hammock which hung from the sides of the stick walls. She smiled as we walked in.

"Do you know where my mom went?" I asked her, noticing that no one else was inside.

"She went to Aunt Cindy's house with your dad and the kids. She said to tell you that you can stay here tonight with us, if you want to."

What I really want is to get the heck out of here, I thought, sitting down on one of the stumps trying to ease my panic.

"What's the matter?" asked Janice, noticing that I wasn't feeling well. "Is the heat getting to you? When we first moved here, the heat made me feel sick too. You should eat something, and then you can shower and go to sleep. You'll feel better in the morning, I promise."

There was no use in trying to explain how I was feeling, so I decided to just go along with her suggestions. And while she hovered over the stove, asking if I wanted some corn tortillas, Katrina sat down at the table with her own plate of food—thoroughly enjoying every bite. But when her sister set my plate of food in front of me it was all I could do not to throw up. "What is this black stuff?" I asked, horrified. "It looks like mashed cockroaches!"

"Beans!" they both shouted at the same time.

"Beans aren't supposed to look like this!" I said, grimacing.

Janice laughed. "We don't have pinto beans down here. The shells are too soft, and weevils love them. These beans have a tough shell that weevils can't get into. They're the only kind of beans you'll be eating from now on."

Not wanting to appear ungrateful, I put a spoonful in my mouth. I could see what she meant by them having unusually tough skin but that wasn't the problem for me. My problem seemed to be my imagination. After so much talk about mosquitoes, spiders, scorpions and tarantulas, I couldn't get my mind to stop imagining the beans as cockroaches—and I couldn't bring myself to eat another bite.

Pushing the plate away, I asked Katrina to loan me some clean clothes to change into and to please walk me out to the shower room. Leaving the kitchen, I thought about Gregario. I hoped he was okay and wished with all my heart that I could get out of here and be with him. Not being able to see him is going to kill me, I thought glumly.

I stood beneath the cake pan showerhead and cried. I could feel the cold water hitting my body, washing away the sweat and tears that were running down my face. "I hate this place!" I said out loud, not caring if anybody heard me. The thought of constantly having to worry about snakes seemed unbearable. The living conditions were horrible—nothing but filth and disease and things that crawled all over you; and the rank smell that hung in the hot, sticky air was sickening. How was I supposed to take care of my siblings and keep Mom's house clean in this environment? I would take Baja-hell over this hell any day!

I tossed and turned all night. The unrelenting heat and the buzzing mosquitoes trying to get through the nets kept me awake. The next morning, I walked to Aunt Cindy's house to find Mom. She had gone somewhere and while I waited for her to come back, I visited with Aunt Cindy's four daughters.

One of them, Becca, said she was hungry and asked me if I wanted to have a cup of atole with her. She offered me a glass filled with a watery substance which I gingerly accepted and hesitantly sipped. It reminded me of watered-down, diluted wheat mush. I sat in their hammock while I finished the drink and looked around at their home. It, too, was made of sticks and had a leaf roof. They had no need for a cinderblock house with real bedrooms because they all slept in a loft above their living space. Aunt Cindy had been living here, and in Belize, for a very long time and all her family was accustomed to the environment. Becca said that cinderblock houses were much too hot to sleep in and that she preferred the cooler stick houses. She agreed that it was easier for snakes and bugs to get in, but said she wasn't bothered by them.

"Would you like to take a tour of the town?" she asked, taking the empty glass from my hand.

I didn't really want to, but I figured I would have to get to know this place eventually, so I agreed and followed her out the door. We walked across the street and stood in front of my aunt's house. My mom's sister, Carla, was married to Floyd, along with Linda—Katrina's mom. Her house was the same as Linda's—having the two separate structures. We continued along the road, stopping at the next house. It was made of cement on the bottom and stick on the top, with a leaf roof. From what I had seen so far, a lot of the homes were built like this one.

Next, she took me to the basketball court and pointed to a house on the corner, asking, "Can you guess whose house that is?"

I knew from the look on her face that this was where we were going to live. It had two structures, but Becca explained that the Mayan's who owned it would be living in the stick house and only lending us the cinderblock house—which was fine with me!

I followed Becca inside and took a quick look around. It was similar to Linda's house, and I wondered how Mom was going to live here with so many kids—nine of us still living with her. I went outside and walked around to the back of the house. It had the same set-up as Linda's house—the one Katrina had shown me yesterday. The outhouse, the shower room—even all the holes in the flimsy, cheap tin—were the same.

I knew I needed to find a way to make the best of this place, because I was sure Dad would not be taking us back to Chihuahua anytime soon. I'm going to clean everything from top to bottom, I decided. I may not be able to do anything about this despicable place or about being poor, but I sure can do something about the filth.

Minutes later, I heard a truck pull up to the house. All my brothers and sisters jumped out, along with my mom and dad. Mom walked into her new home and looked around. With the help of my brothers and sisters, Dad unloaded the truck—piling everything in a corner of our new house. We had no furniture, so moving-in didn't take long, and I wondered where we were going to sit, eat, and sleep without so much as a chair.

Later that day, Mom told me that we would soon have bed frames, which were being made for us by Uncle George, and she would need to get mattresses for them. "Dad and I are going into the city tomorrow," she said. "Grandma gave me some money to buy a few things for our new home, and your dad wants to take me to get the shopping done before he leaves. He's heading back to Chihuahua to get the rest of the family."

Anticipating the arrival of real beds soon, we spent the first night in our new home sleeping on the floor. The heat was unbearable along with the mosquitoes feasting on our flesh. I got up several times during the night, taking my younger sisters with me to cool down with a cold shower. I could not believe we were stuck in a place like this, but there was absolutely nothing I could do about it, so I focused instead on the fans Mom told me she would be buying.

Aunt Cindy was so sweet, preparing meals for us until Mom and Dad came back from the city. When they finally returned, Mom said they had shopped at a Mexican furniture store—one that obviously did not sell very good merchandise. As I helped unload the truck, I could tell that the chairs and mattresses were not going to withstand much use. Especially the kind of use they would be getting from our big family!

We unloaded a small stove, a refrigerator, eight chairs, three mattresses, and two oscillating fans—which were an absolute blessing, so I wasn't about to complain about their quality! (Eventually, Uncle George made us a table, some shelves for clothes, and a frame for a sink in our tiny kitchen; and Mom hung a few crates on the walls to use for storing things like salt, oil and sugar.)

After we were somewhat settled in our new home, Mom drove Dad back into the city so he could catch the bus to Chihuahua—leaving the truck for my mom to use while he was away.

Life was extremely rough in this part of Mexico. A native plant called Chechen, meaning poison sumac, grew everywhere. I hadn't yet learned how to distinguish these plants from other plants and was constantly getting burned—leaving huge blisters on my legs and shins, as if somebody had thrown boiling water on me.

I did all the laundry by hand on a scrub board, and my hands would often break out in blisters too, because whenever we were outside our clothes invariably made contact with the poisonous plants. There were even times when I wiped the sweat off my brow, not knowing that I had sumac on my hands, and would end up burning my face.

Having stomach aches and diarrhea became second nature to me—and the deworming process we went through every few months proved to be a complete waste of time. I also became acquainted with another little pest which I added to the long list of hellish critters. One day, while walking home from Aunt Cindy's house, I took the shortcut through the bushes growing in the field by the basketball court. The following day, I noticed hundreds of little welts all around my waist, thighs, knees, armpits and even on the nipples of my developing breasts. The welts itched horribly, so after showering and not getting any relief, I decided to share my embarrassing dilemma with Mom.

"They're chiggers," she said, "and you can't see them unless you're in direct sunlight. They're red and as small as the tip of a pin. Whenever you walk in any sort of brush, you need to shower immediately. So go out to the shower room right now. In the bright sunlight maybe you'll be able to see them and dig them out with a needle."

I did as she told me, but with all the scratching I had done I could see nothing but red sores. She had also said that if I couldn't dig them out, I could smother them with nail polish. So, that was next; and putting nail polish on the sores stung like crazy! But I wanted them gone, so from then on, nail polish became an important part of my daily staying-alive-and-well routine. And, depending on the color of the polish, I walked around with purple, pink and gray spots most of the time—although I eventually figured out how to avoid the polka dot look, and asked Mom to buy me a bottle of clear polish!

Along with the unrelenting heat, mosquitoes, snakes, bugs, worms, lack of social events and finances, there was the loneliness... I missed Gregario and the large family my father had created—all his wives and their children, my half-brothers and sisters. I kept waiting for Dad to return with them, but that day never came. He would come down to see us every six months or so, but he was always alone... His visits were short—never more than five or six days—and he spent most of those days in meetings with Floyd; visiting us only in the evenings. I had a lot of questions for him about the family, but I didn't dare ask him why he had not moved them down here yet. Instead, I tried to stay optimistic, telling myself that someday they would arrive.

The hope of our family being together again gave me strength in my moments of weakness. The misery of this God forsaken place, and the life I was living here, was hard to go through on my own; and I wished that all my half-brothers and sisters were here with me. I missed them all so much!

For now, the highlights of my life were playing basketball in the evenings with a few of the cousins, occasionally taking the bus to Cancún to visit my half-sister, Alondra, and waiting for Mom to come back from town after Dad wired her money for groceries. He couldn't afford to send much, nor did he send it very often, but when he did it felt like Christmas, or what I imagined Christmas must feel like—and I could only imagine it because we were forbidden to celebrate it. During the long stretches of time when Dad didn't send us money, Floyd's group would help us however they could. And, sometimes, if they were able to afford it, they would loan Mom money to get us by.

CHAPTER TEN

WAITING BY THE ENTRANCE

Within my heart live two religions: Happiness and Sadness. And as I get closer to one, the other disappears.

One afternoon, Mom and I—along with the kids—were sitting at the table eating beans and tortillas. I noticed a little white truck pull up to our house. A man got out and made his way to our front door. Mom quickly got up and walked outside to greet him. I watched as the man said something to her while handing her a piece of paper. Mom took the paper, looked down at it, then nodded her head. They exchanged a few more words before the man got back in his truck and she came back into the house.

As Mom walked through the door she said, "I have to go into town right now. This is a message that your dad will be calling me in a few hours at the pay phone in town. It says 'urgent' on it, so I need to make sure to be there. Please keep an eye on the kids, Vera, I'll be back in a while," she added, grabbing her purse and keys, then running out to the truck.

Watching the kids felt normal to me. I did it even when Mom was home, so after she left, I continued with my standard routine of feeding, bathing and playing with my brothers and sisters. Mom returned just as it was getting dark, and as soon as she came through the door, I knew something was terribly wrong. Her eyes were swollen, and she looked devastated.

"Mom, what is it?" I asked, noticing that she had not brought anything in from the truck, which meant that the call was not about receiving money.

"It's Amy," she said, tears running down her face. "Amy and Samuel's sister were in a terrible car accident. Both have died."

I felt a cold chill run up and down my spine. I couldn't believe what I was hearing! Amy? Dead? This can't be real, I thought... I sat down on the closest chair, trying to steady my trembling legs as my mind raced with questions: How did this happen? Who was driving? What about her children? What about Samuel?

I began spewing out questions, one right after the other, hardly waiting for responses, but Mom didn't have a lot of answers. All she knew was that Amy was driving with Samuel's sister. A semi-truck ran her off the road causing her car to roll, which killed them both.

Mom was leaving immediately, going back to Chihuahua for a week taking only my baby sister with her. I would be staying home to look after the other kids. My older brother, Edwin—who was fifteen—had recently started working in town at a hotel as a bellboy. Dad was sending money less and less often and Mom needed Edwin's paycheck to help keep us fed, so he would not be able to stay home and help me. "But he will be your go-to contact if you need anything," she said.

"Why can't I go with you?" I asked, as a feeling of emptiness and devastation began to overtake my heart. "Please don't leave me here! Take me with you," I begged, even though I knew there was no way she could afford it.

"I wish I could," she said, as more tears poured from her eyes. "I had to ask Grandma for help again. Do you know how humiliating it is to have to get money from my mother all the time when I have a husband who should be providing for me?"

I hadn't realized she felt this way and was surprised to learn that constantly depending on Grandma for financial help was humiliating for her. I could tell she was torn between wanting to go to the funeral and not wanting to ask Grandma for more money. I suddenly sensed her loneliness, and it dawned on me that not only had I been missing our family, but that Mom had been missing them too. I could see how being neglected by Dad was causing her pain. It was written all over her face and suddenly my heart ached for her. Our living conditions were tough and trying to take care of nine children on her own, without Dad's help, along with feeling lonely and lost in her situation, was taking its toll on her.

Floyd was still claiming to be a messenger, and most of his followers were related to his wife, Carla—one of my mom's sisters. Mom had agreed to move down here believing that eventually Dad would move the rest of the family here and we would all follow Floyd. But it still had not happened, and it left Mom feeling abandoned, betrayed, and torn between families. She wanted to be here with her own family, and yet she also wanted to go back to Chihuahua and be part of her husband's family. But even if she chose Chihuahua, we couldn't afford to move back there—so there really was no decision to be made.

"Everything's going to be okay, Vera," she said, wiping her eyes with the back of her hand.

The shock of Amy's death had unleashed a whole new flow of sadness within her. One, that until now, I didn't even know existed... I watched as she did her best to gain control of her feelings. "Life isn't always easy," she continued, picking up a dirty shirt from the floor and blowing her nose into it. "Sometimes we don't understand why things are the way they are. We just have to trust God. He knows what is best for us and we don't get to decide what that is. We just have to be strong. And I need you to be strong. I know you'll take good care of the house and kids while I'm away, and I promise to take lots of pictures to bring back and share with you."

As she hurried about, preparing for her trip, I sat on the chair for the longest time. I thought about Amy and her children. She had three of them now, a boy and two girls. I wondered who was going to take care of them now that they had no mother. I thought about Mom and Dad, too, wondering why Dad still hadn't moved the rest of the family here—but knowing it was not a good time to ask Mom about it. I thought about God. I wondered why he expected my mom to suffer so much; why he loved his sons more than his daughters; and why women couldn't make it to heaven without men. And, because Samuel was still alive, I wondered if that meant Amy was not in heaven. Maybe she has to wait by the entrance, I thought— until he dies, and then she can go in, or maybe she is in hell because she died first. The thought of hell made me shiver, but my heart somehow knew that she was not in hell, and I liked the thought of her waiting for Samuel by the entrance so much more than her facing the flames of purgatory.

The following week seemed to drag on forever. Amy's death stole its way into all my thoughts, and memories of her constantly flooded my mind. I filled the long days with housecleaning, laundry, meals, and showers for my siblings. Every evening I would make popcorn that I'd borrowed from my aunt and we would sit around the table playing games. And, when they were finally tired, I'd pray with them and put them all to bed, then crawl into bed myself— physically exhausted, sending my own prayers to God... A God I knew had no use for me, a girl. A God whom I was sure had better things to do than listen to my prayers. But even though I constantly struggled with my own feelings of unworthiness, I never gave up on praying to him—believing with all my heart that one day I would make him very proud of me. So, every night before drifting off to sleep, I whispered, "Someday I will gain your love, God... Someday."

CHAPTER ELEVEN

I WANTED TO JUMP INTO THE GRAVE WITH HER

Out of this world and into the grave… Perhaps death is how beautiful souls remind us to live each day as if it were our last.

Mom was coming home today, and I looked forward to her lifting the burden of so much responsibility from my shoulders. I was also looking forward to having an adult in the house at night again. It was a little scary knowing that if something happened during the night, and I needed help, I would have to walk to Aunt Cindy's house in the dark—snakes everywhere!

I was in the outhouse when Mom and my youngest sister finally got home. It felt like they had been gone for a month rather than only a week, and as soon as I heard the truck I ran down the trail, into the house—scooped up my baby sister, held her in my arms, and kissed and hugged her tightly. I had missed her so much! Mom looked a little more at peace than she had the day she left. She hugged me as she asked how everything went.

"Everything went well, except it felt like you were gone forever," I answered, as she began rummaging through all the things she had brought home—including a thirteen-inch black-and-white TV, an old VCR, and some movies. All the kids gathered around her, ecstatic when they saw the TV.

"Can we watch it?" they asked, jumping up and down. "Can we watch it right now? Pleeeease."

"Not yet," Mom said. "Maybe later this evening."

The kids sulked for a few minutes, then went outside as Mom continued to go through her pile of stuff. She finally found what she was looking for and handed it to me. It was a white envelope filled with pictures she had taken, just as she had promised. I immediately sat down in the middle of the floor and pulled the pictures out of the envelope. Countless photos of all the family at the funeral, and a picture that broke my heart the second I saw it... It was Samuel standing next to a pile of dirt—Amy's grave, covered with flowers. He was holding their baby girl, Elise, in one arm; while their son and oldest daughter, Andrew and Alice, stood at his sides clutching his legs.

I stared at the picture for a long time... As I looked at Samuel's face, I saw immense pain in his eyes and an overwhelming feeling of empathy took over my being. I felt a strong desire to take that pain away from him, and when I looked at Amy's children, my eyes filled with tears. Something in my chest felt like it was being ripped apart. I quickly put the pictures back into the envelope and tried to steady my breathing.

That was a family picture, I said to myself... But now, a pile of dirt is all that is left of Amy... Death felt so frightening to me in that moment. I imagined myself as Amy, all alone, buried in a deep hole—no longer able to hold her children. Sadly, I wondered what was going to happen to them, and who was going to make sure they were safe. I imagined how lonely she must feel in that grave and, suddenly, I wanted to jump into the grave with her! I wanted to stay with her at night so she wouldn't be scared. I wanted to comfort her and bring her food in case she got hungry. I wanted to do whatever I could to make her feel better. In my head, I knew I couldn't do these things for her because she was no longer alive, but in my heart, I desperately wanted to. Then, out of nowhere, my desperation turned to hope—lighting me up like a ray of sunshine. I suddenly knew exactly what I could do. I could shower her children with love when I moved back to Chihuahua to marry Gregario!

I pulled the picture out of the envelope and lightly touched Amy's grave with my fingertips. Next, I gently touched her children's faces as I ever so softly said the words, "I love you." Then, looking upward and closing my eyes, I imagined her and her smile as I whispered those words again.

In my heart, I knew she heard me, and I felt at peace as I sensed the never-ending flow of her love.

CHAPTER TWELVE

MAYBE I'M STILL A VIRGIN

Stench is not a word commonly used to describe rape, but if I were in charge of definitions, I would certainly add it to the list—and I would put it at the top. Not only does it look ugly, sound ugly, and feel ugly—it also smells ugly. It is a putrid odor that clings to the skin and no matter how many times you try to wash it off—or how hard you scrub—it remains, emanating from every part of you while it slowly permeates your heart. And what, exactly, does rape smell like? It smells like shame.

It has now been eighteen months since Amy's death... Dad told me that her children were living with Samuel's second wife, Stella, and that they were finally starting to adapt to the loss of their mother, or so it seemed.

Dad's visits dwindled, each lasting only a few days—with five or six months between them—but Mom has finally shared the truth with me: He is no longer planning on moving the rest of the family here. He believes that Jerome was a true prophet of God, but he's not quite sure that Floyd is a true messenger of God. And, because of his uncertainty, he thinks he'll be better off keeping the rest of his wives and children in Chihuahua. The saddest part of all, is that both Mom and Dad agreed that Mom should stay here and keep paving the way for the family in case Dad changes his mind about Floyd.

Even though this is devastating news to me, I'm not at all surprised. Mom seems to think that doing what is right is all about sacrificing, and there's plenty of that going on around here. Although, surrounded by her own family, it appears she is finding fulfillment. I believe it may be the glue that is holding her together in this hellish, poverty-stricken place. That, and Grandma sending her money more often. If not for her generosity, we would have starved while waiting for Dad to send a few pesos... I don't know how he sleeps at night knowing his children may be going to bed hungry. But without answers or options, I settle into a life of survival and accept the idea that my dad is just a visiting father who must go home to his permanent family. I still feel fearful whenever I'm around him and, truthfully, I'm perfectly fine with his quick and only occasional visits—it's his wives and my half-brothers and sisters that I don't like living without.

Whenever Dad comes to visit, he puts the fear of hell into me. The destruction of the United States, the wickedness of our people, and the shame that we all should be feeling for not doing what God requires of us are things he constantly talks about. Not surprising that after his fire-and-brimstone preaching, I'm always left feeling like there is no hope for me. I walk around feeling a sense of doom and gloom—sure that the devil's inferno is just around the corner waiting for me. But, being a fixer, one day after Dad left, I decided to sit down with a piece of paper and a pen and map out exactly what I needed to do to get to Heaven. I wanted to fix this doom and gloom feeling once and for all! I did not want to be one of the many that God was angry and disappointed with, or one he sent straight to hell by wiping them off the face of the Earth, like Dad said he would.

As I sat staring at the blank sheet of paper, I wondered what I could do to save myself... I wrestled with what I wanted to write versus what I thought God would want me to write. In all honesty, I wanted to write: *I will love everyone. I will buy them all food. I will tell everyone they are special.* But I knew those things were silly, so I wrote instead: *I will follow the Ten Commandments. I will listen to what Dad has taught me about the prophets and be an obedient daughter. I will live celestial marriage.* I will do these things, I decided, as I folded the piece of paper and tucked it into my pocket.

Later that evening I took the *Book of Mormon* with me to bed. I was determined to start at the beginning and read a few verses every night before going to sleep. I'm going to make it to Heaven, I thought. I'm going to make it, come heck or high water!

I continued to feel lonely in our jungle home in Quintana-roo and looked forward to occasional visits with my half-sister, Alondra, in Cancún. She was the daughter of one of Dad's Mexican wives and was always happy to see me, although Mom didn't let me go very often because she felt lost without my help whenever I was away.

Alondra was very lonely because her husband, Wade, spent most of his time with his first wife and very little time with her. But, regardless of how much he neglected her, he was a very possessive and jealous man. He didn't like Alondra talking to anyone— especially her neighbors—and he didn't like her having any friends. Although, whenever Dad traveled from Chihuahua, he always stopped and visited her on his way to Quintana-roo. And whenever I could, I went to visit her too.

Alondra was raised the same way I was and knew the importance of celestial marriage. When she was sixteen and married Wade, he was a devout Catholic with a wife and children. He exploited the fact that Alondra was willing to marry an already married man, purposely letting her believe she was living celestial marriage. In his and his Catholic wife's mind, she was nothing but a mistress. She became a possession of his and the way he treated her reflected it.

Once, I witnessed how enraged he became when he drove up to her house and caught her speaking to one of the neighbors. Alondra ran into the house, then fled to her bedroom—Wade, like a mad dog, right behind her. He slammed the bedroom door shut, and I could hear her crying as he blasted her with hostile words. Knowing how vicious he could be, I wondered if I should just leave, but I knew Alondra would be sad if I did and I couldn't leave José—her two-year-old son—in the front room by himself. Not knowing what else to do, I turned up the volume of the TV so little José didn't have to hear his mom cry. A few minutes later, Wade and Alondra emerged from the room holding hands—Alondra, wearing a plastic smile, pretending everything was fine.

She walked over and sat next to me on the couch, putting her arm around me and thanking me for coming to see her. I smiled at her as she pointed at my leg and said, "Ouch, Vera, what happened to you?"

I had accidentally gotten into poison sumac again and had several large burns on my calf and thigh. "Just a few burns from Chechen again," I said quietly.

Concerned, Alondra looked up at Wade and asked him to come closer and look at the blisters on my legs.

Coming much closer than he needed to, Wade's beady eyes roved all the way up my thighs, then paused for a second before meandering their way back down. His look made me extremely uncomfortable, but I didn't really know why... Perhaps because it reminded me of the way I felt when the crude stranger with the apples had kissed me. Or, maybe the strange feeling I had was my soul's way of telling me to stay away from the man with the roving eyes. Confused by Wade's odd behavior, I didn't know which one it was—but I did know that I couldn't listen to the voice within me and follow the rules of Dad's God at the same time, so I chose to disregard what might be the voice of my own soul, certain that if it *were* speaking to me, it must be wrong.

The next time I visited Alondra, we spent our time together laughing and playing board games. She made delicious Mexican meals with steak and chicken and all the types of food that we could not afford to eat at our house. We ate cookies and ice cream galore while watching Mexican soap operas and other shows on her color TV.

We always had such a good time together but whenever Wade came around, she seemed like a different person. I sensed a deep sadness in her that she somehow managed to keep hidden from the world. And, on the nights that Wade didn't sleep at her house and was with his other wife, we would talk most of the night and I would always fall asleep in her bed.

One evening while Wade was with Alondra in her room, I fell asleep on the living room floor but was suddenly awakened in the middle of the night by someone rubbing my behind. Sleepy and confused, I thought little José might be trying to wake me up but when I turned over to see if it was him, I was shocked to see Wade kneeling beside me! I instantly jumped up—and he quickly left the room.

A familiar feeling arose within me—the one I always had when something didn't seem right. Feeling uneasy, I wrapped the sheet around myself and laid down on the couch. Closing my eyes, I buried that ever-familiar feeling by reasoning my way out of it... Maybe men have a right to rub my behind, I thought. After all, they do own women... I tried to imagine what Dad would say if I complained to him about it and immediately pictured his response. It wasn't in my favor.

I really didn't know anything about men—or their private worlds—but what I did know was that I never had that uneasy feeling around Gregario. Nevertheless, I tried convincing myself that

Wade touching me didn't mean anything, and I had no reason to feel uncomfortable. And by the time I got back home the next day, I had decided that my feelings of discomfort were the work of the devil—and I should not pay any attention to them.

My next visit with Alondra was for the birth of her daughter, Rosa. I had just turned sixteen, and Mom had agreed to let me spend a few weeks with her so I could help out after the delivery... Wade came and went in the days before Alondra gave birth to their second child—and, to my relief, he didn't do anything that made me feel uncomfortable. Everything seemed to be fine and when Alondra went into labor, I stayed at the house keeping an eye on José while she and Wade were at the hospital.

The next morning Wade stopped by the house to let me know the baby had come and that she and Alondra were doing well. He grabbed some clothes and a few things for the baby, then said he was going back to the hospital, adding that he would be bringing Alondra and the baby home later in the day.

When they arrived, I had dinner waiting for them and, after Alondra had eaten and I'd tucked her into bed, Wade headed out the door, saying he'd be back tomorrow.

After little José and the baby went to sleep, I crawled into bed with Alondra and we talked until we both fell asleep. But a few hours later, I was awakened by a strange feeling—someone was tugging at my underwear! Startled, I opened my eyes and found that Wade had returned and had wedged himself between Alondra and me. The look in his eyes frightened me and when he pulled his hand back, I jumped up and ran into the living room.

Feeling angry, scared and confused all at the same time, there was no way I could talk myself into believing that this was the right way for any man to act—especially Alondra's husband. It was wrong—very wrong—and he knew it!

The following afternoon, while Alondra was taking a nap, Wade barged into the front room where I was watching television.

"Can we step outside for a minute?" he asked. "I need to talk to you."

Anxious to hear his apology—and expecting it—I followed him outside.

"Listen," he said, "I like you a lot and I've convinced Alondra to let me marry you."

"What?" I said, stunned by his words. "Marry you... Are you kidding me?"

Daring to look into his eyes, I gave him a disgusted look, then continued, "First of all, you are a Catholic and I'm smart enough to know that Catholics don't live plural marriage. Alondra believes she's living celestial marriage with you and she loves you, but you and your wife both know that she's nothing more than your mistress! I would never marry you, Wade. Never!"

His angry eyes turned into daggers as he thrust the same piercing glare into me that I'd seen him use on Alondra many times—the one that sent shivers down my spine... I know I must live celestial marriage to make it into God's Kingdom, I thought, but I'm *not* required to live it with a Catholic! An abusive, revolting Catholic, I added silently, turning around and going back to the house.

Gathering up the plates and taking them to the sink after we'd finished dinner that evening, Wade followed me into the kitchen. Then, coming much too close for comfort, he whispered something into my ear before disappearing into Alondra's room and closing the door... "You're a little star in the sky," he said jeeringly, "and you think I cannot have you. But one day you *will* be mine."

The next morning, while I was sorting dirty laundry—intending to do Alondra's wash—Wade came out of the bedroom. "You can put all that back in the hamper," he said. "We're taking the laundry to my parent's house. They have an electric washer we can use, and it's much faster than doing it by hand."

I had been to his parent's house many times with Alondra. They owned a grocery store with a small apartment above it, and the washer was located on the veranda. Alondra often shopped and visited with them in the store while she did her laundry. So, because it was not unusual to do laundry there, I put all the dirty laundry back into the hampers—then kept myself busy cleaning while waiting for Alondra to get ready.

Wondering what was taking her so long, I poked my head through the open door of her room to see if she needed help with anything. But she wasn't getting ready, she was sitting on her bed next to Wade, holding her baby. Looking tired, she smiled at me and said, "Wade thinks it would be better for me to stay here and take a nap while you guys go and get the laundry done."

I'm not going with him by myself, I thought—but quickly erased it from my mind when she added, "José can go with you. That way I can take a good nap."

I breathed a sigh of relief knowing that I wouldn't be going with Wade alone. Then, I loaded all the hampers into the back of the car and after putting José in the front seat, I hopped into the back. Wade didn't say a word as he got into the driver's seat and we drove off.

When we arrived at his parent's house, his mother greeted me warmly, then helped me carry the hampers upstairs to the veranda. She showed me how to use the washing machine, letting me know she'd be in the store if I needed anything.

Wade stayed downstairs in the store visiting with the customers while looking after little José. Happy that he was leaving me alone, I washed the first load and hung it out to dry. While waiting for the second load to be done, I went into the little room off the veranda where there was a bed and a hammock. A cool breeze floated through the open windows and doors, and it felt heavenly! My fear of waking up next to Wade again made it impossible for me to get a good night's sleep at Alondra's house and left me feeling exhausted, so I laid down on the bed and closed my eyes.

I felt safer here, with Wade's family around me—sure that he wouldn't dream of touching me while they were around. He hadn't done or said anything to me all morning and he seemed to be content staying downstairs in the store, so I let myself drift off to sleep—the gentle breeze calming my soul as I curled up on the soft bed.

Suddenly, I felt a heaviness on top of me—the weight of the man who thoroughly disgusted me! I knew it was Wade before I even opened my eyes and, clinging to the hope that he would disappear as soon as he was discovered, I put my hands on his chest and tried to push him away. But he was so much bigger and stronger than I was, and no matter how hard I pushed, I couldn't get him off me.

He grabbed both my arms, pinning them above my head with one hand as he reached up the side of my baggy shorts and began probing me with the other. His fingers inside of me sent a frantic blast of desperation through me and I fought like a wildcat to get away from him—but the harder I fought, the more determined he became; and it only made him tighten his grasp on my arms.

"Unreachable little star, unreachable little star," he kept saying—glaring into my frightened eyes while pushing his fingers into me.

My world was exploding—the world where I was innocent, the world where I was safe. The world that I didn't always like, but other than one disgustingly gross kiss from a derelict with a bag of apples, it was a world where my young body had never been touched inappropriately nor violated by a man. My mind reeled with dark thoughts, terrified of what he might do next as every inch of me struggled to free myself from his iron grip. Then, suddenly, I thought I had done it—he withdrew his wicked fingers, and I was sure he was going to let go of me, but I was wrong.

He lifted himself off me just enough to unzip his pants, then I felt his penis brush against me and, bulging with repulsive desire, he tried to force his way into me. I was too shocked and too afraid to cry out, so I squeezed my eyes shut—praying that it was only a bad dream. But the harder he pushed, the more it hurt and the more real it became. A silent scream erupted from my soul, begging him to stop—pleading with the man-god to have mercy for the girl who was where she was because she wanted to help her half-sister.

I held my breath, clenched my teeth and kept my eyes squeezed shut as he heaved himself into me—but suddenly stopped, let me go, jumped to his feet, and zipped up his pants with lightning speed.

Free at last, I flew out of the room—back to the veranda—almost colliding with his mother who was bent over the washing machine. She had come upstairs to see if I needed help with the laundry, and I did need help—but not with the dirty clothes. I needed help with her dirty son, his dirty games, and his filthy, vile ways.

Wade must have seen her through the door and not wanting to get caught he had let me go and quickly zipped up his pants. So grateful to be saved by her, I helped her take the clothes out of the washer, then smiled and thanked her.

She smiled back at me. "No problem," she said.

I knew she assumed I was thanking her for helping me with the wash, because only I knew the real reason for my gratitude. But it didn't matter—she had come upstairs. She had saved me from her evil son. And I had never been so grateful to anyone in my life.

Wade disappeared down the stairs and I made a vow to myself that I would *never* stay at Alondra's house again. As much as I loved her, and as sad as it was to even think about never visiting her again, having to deal with her husband's vile sexual advances and vulgar ways was just too frightening. The man was a monster. A selfish, heartless, perverted monster.

Dad would be arriving in two days. He was flying into Cancún from Chihuahua and would be stopping to visit Alondra before heading to Quintana-roo for his usual five-day visit. And, thank God, I would be going back with him… It was the first time in my life that I was anxious to see him. As far as I was concerned, he couldn't get here fast enough, because two more days of Wade was two more days too many—and I could not wait to get away from him.

The next forty-eight hours felt like an eternity… I made sure to have little José with me everywhere I went, and I didn't sleep a wink while I waited for Dad. I tried to keep my mind busy so I wouldn't think about what had happened, but at night my thoughts would get away from me. I found myself trying to make sense of it all. Trying to justify it. Trying to reason my way through it. And, in some sort of twisted way, I convinced myself that it was my own fault… If only I had not gone to do the laundry with him. If only I had not come to Cancún. If only this, if only that—my mind kept spinning it round and round—but most of my thoughts were about one thing: I didn't know if what Wade had done to me was considered having sex with him or not. Actually, I knew very little about sex; therefore, I didn't know if I was a virgin anymore—and this thought haunted me. Getting married as a virgin was an important part of my religious upbringing. What if I was no longer chaste and Gregario didn't want me? What if no man wanted me because I wasn't pure? I could never live celestial marriage and would be left to roam with the devil in hell forever!

I remembered a conversation I'd had at a sleepover with Janice. She knew more about sex than I did because she dared to ask her married sister questions about the forbidden topic, and she had told me what they'd talked about—letting me know that sex is when a man puts his penis in a girl, adding, "And it hurts really, really bad and makes you bleed."

I had asked her how long they have to leave their penis in us, and she wasn't sure but said she thought that maybe they had to leave it in all night. As I recalled this conversation, I felt a little better… Maybe I'm still a virgin, I thought hopefully. Wade didn't pin me down all night, there was no blood, and even though he forced his way into me, he let me go right after the first painful thrust... Oh, I hope so... Please let me still be a virgin, I prayed silently—I feel like damaged goods, but please don't let it be true.

CHAPTER THIRTEEN

HER DREAM

It was hard for me to imagine, and even though I could not put it into words, it amazed me that a man as seemingly holy as my father could believe the dark lies of another man. Had he really been fooled by a sinner? Or, perhaps, was he blinded by the bright possibility of one less girl to feed?... I am ashamed to even think that my father could be so weak, but would not God also conclude that our blindness is most apparent when we are standing in the light?

Dad finally arrived, and after a short visit with Alondra, he asked me if I was ready to head out.

I've been packed and ready to go for longer than you will ever know, I thought, simply nodding my head—trying to hide my enthusiasm about leaving.

Dad stood up, but before he could say goodbye, Wade offered to give us a ride home.

"I can't let you take the bus," he said. "I will gladly take you and your daughter home."

Oh, crap, I thought, this is going to be an eternal three-hour drive!

Dad seemed to have a good relationship with the lecherous monster and bought into all his fake charm. The phony respect and admiration he showed my father was only because Dad had allowed him, a married Catholic man, to have one of his beautiful daughters.

Dad certainly believed that celestial marriage was one of the most important principles Jerome taught, but he also believed that all men—regardless of their religion—were meant to have more than one wife. This is how he justified the marriage that should have never been, but poor Alondra was being made a fool of. She truly believed she had the key to Heaven because she was living celestial marriage. But both she and my father had been tricked by a man with a scam—a Catholic who hid his sins beneath a confession of lies by pretending he honored our way of life.

It was hard for me to imagine—my father, holy as he was, being fooled by a sinner... Wade repulsed me. His mere existence made me angry, and the things he did hurt me deeply—not just the things he did to me, but also the way he treated Alondra. He took advantage of her by exploiting her religious upbringing, then kept her prisoner by isolating her from anyone who might help her see the truth. He allowed her to spend time with me, which brought her so much joy, but it wasn't for the sake of her happiness—it was for the sake of his own selfish, carnal desires. My relationship with my half-sister would never be the same because of the secret I had to keep from her and, sadly, I said goodbye, knowing I would never go back to her house to visit her again.

We arrived home and after unloading my bags and hugging Mom and the kids, I went straight to the shower room. I hadn't been able to shower for the last two days for fear that Wade might barge into the bathroom, catching me undressed and alone. Now, feeling safe, I began to undress, and as I turned the water on, for the first time in my life I felt disgusted in my own body. I wanted so desperately to feel clean again, to wash the feeling of Wade's wicked hands off my body, but I felt dirty and no matter how much soap and water I used I could not rid myself of his ugly invasion of my innocence. I stood under that water for the longest time trying to scrub away what had already sunk into my bones and become part of me.

Suddenly, I heard Mom's voice asking me if I was okay.

"Yes," I answered quickly—finally turning off the water and grabbing a towel.

"I was just checking," she said. "You've been in there for over an hour."

"I'm fine, Mom, thanks," I said—secretly hoping I was as clean on the inside as I was on the outside, but still feeling the filth under my skin.

Luckily, Wade returned to Cancún shortly after taking us home and, a few days later, I found Dad sitting at the kitchen table—alone—drinking coffee. Mom was on her morning walk with Aunt Cindy and as I began cleaning up the breakfast dishes, I noticed Dad staring at me with a hint of mild astonishment in his eyes. It had been eight months since his last visit and I had physically matured a lot during that time but, until now, I don't think he noticed that I was no longer a little girl.

"You're getting all grown up, sister," he said, taking a sip of coffee. "You know, one of the Saunders boys was heading down here to see you a couple of weeks ago but the bus he was on crashed and rolled over. He was hoping to get to know you, and he sure was disappointed that he never made it down here."

A Saunders boy, I thought, giving Dad a nervous smile… There were so many Saunders boys, and I wondered which one it could be. Gregario was a Saunders boy, but he didn't go by that last name, so I knew it couldn't be him—which made my heart sink because he was the only boy I would be interested in seeing. This wasn't the first time I'd heard about the Saunders boys wanting to come down here to check out the young girls as though we were a bunch of cattle to be picked over.

Interrupting my thoughts, Mom suddenly walked into the kitchen and sat down next to Dad.

"I was just telling Vera how grown up she is," said Dad.

Nodding her head in agreement, Mom winked at me and smiled, saying, "She sure is!"

I wondered if she could tell how different I felt after returning from my stay at Alondra's house—praying to God that she couldn't. And, without a word, I finished the dishes then wandered into my room and sat on the edge of the bed—trying to figure out which Saunders boy Dad had been talking about.

As if she knew something was up, Mom came into my room. "What's the matter with you, Vera?" she asked.

"Nothing, Mom. Why do think something's the matter with me?"

"This is why I don't like you going to Cancún very often. You always come back with a bad attitude and act like you hate it here. It takes days for you to snap out of it and get back into the swing of life. I'm not going to let you go again for a long, long time," she said, walking out of the room.

After she left, I tried hard to hold back my tears. I wanted to tell her that it wasn't what she was thinking, and that Wade had assaulted me—but I just couldn't find the courage to tell her.

A half-hour later, she came back into the room and sat on the bed next to me. Noticing my tears, she asked, "What's the matter, Vera? Are you upset because I said you're not going to Cancún anymore?"

"No," I answered.

"Then what is it? You've been walking around like somebody died ever since you got home. What's going on?"

I wanted to tell her everything, but I was too embarrassed. Even my period, which had suddenly appeared a few years ago, had been too embarrassing to talk about—and just the thought of talking to her about sex was even more embarrassing. Besides, I didn't even know if Wade had actually had sex with me, so I decided to divulge only half my secret, suddenly blurting out, "Wade asked me to marry him!"

Before I could say anything more, she put her head down and muttered, "That's enough to make me want to throw up."

She seemed thoroughly disgusted. And I had not a single doubt that she was, because she had talked to me often about her disdain for Wade and how he exploited Alondra, saying, "It is not an example of true celestial marriage. It is all about Wade looking out for himself and fulfilling his own ungodly desires."

Finally lifting her head, Mom asked me what I had said when he asked me to marry him—obviously concerned that I might have told him I would.

I wanted to tell her that I had said no but then he had sex with me, but instead I said, "I told him no, I would never marry him—but then he kissed me."

"That son of a gun," she said, with a faraway look in her eyes.

I knew she was worried about me, and a warm feeling of safety engulfed me as I realized that marrying Wade was not something she would ever let happen. I felt better having shared with her even just a little of what he had done to me—and at the same time, I felt worse. Only telling her half my secret left me longing to feel understood, to share the pain and the shame.

Mom put her arm around my shoulder, saying, "I'm glad you told him no. You did the right thing."

Later that evening, after supper was over and I had finished my nightly chores, I sank into our hammock—laying back, feeling somewhat at peace. Eventually, I drifted off to sleep but was suddenly awakened by the sound of Mom's voice… "You can't sleep all night in the hammock, Vera, let's get you to bed."

I stood up, more asleep than awake, as she took my hand and guided me to my bed.

"What time is it?" I asked her.

"It's three in the morning. I had a dream that woke me, and I happened to notice you sleeping in the hammock. Go back to sleep, I'll share my dream with you tomorrow."

When I awoke in the morning, my back ached from falling asleep in the hammock. After taking a few minutes to stretch, I carefully put one foot in front of the other—slowly moving toward the kitchen for breakfast. Mom and the kids were sitting around the table drinking atole and talking with Dad. The mood seemed light and humorous.

Mom smiled at me. "Good morning," she said, as I shuffled my way to the stove, poured myself a cup of watered-down mush, then sat down next to my siblings.

Dad was busy sharing funny stories about his life as a child, and it was nice to hear the lighter side of him for a change. God only knows, I had heard enough of his preaching in the last few days to last me a lifetime—to say nothing of him always trying to cram an endless stream of dark beliefs about God, the gospel, the prophets and the end times into our heads during the rare five days he spent with us every eight months. And, I can honestly say, in those five fire-and-brimstone days, there was absolutely nothing to laugh about. So I liked his lighter mood, noticing that Mom seemed uplifted by it too. But was it really because of Dad, I wondered, or was it something else that had her feeling happier this morning?

I finished my breakfast, and after doing the dishes I headed for the backyard to do the laundry—which meant I would be hauling water, filling tubs, then scrubbing each piece of clothing by hand. It looked like it was going to rain and if I didn't hurry and get everything washed and hung on the clothesline before the rain came, we might not have anything to wear tomorrow.

My knuckles rubbed raw, I had just finished scrubbing the last huge pile of laundry when Mom joined me outside. Helping me fill up the clothesline again, she asked me how I was doing.

"I'm doing good," I said, continuing to hang the clothes.

"You know," she said nonchalantly, "last night I had a dream about you."

"About me?" I asked—surprised that the dream she'd mentioned last night was about me.

"Yes, it was about you—and, well… Samuel."

Suddenly curious, I asked her what she had dreamed.

"I was at your wedding in my dream, and you were marrying Samuel."

"Amy's Samuel?" I asked, laughing at the mere thought of it.

"Yes," she answered.

"That must have been a funny dream," I said, still laughing, but noticing that she didn't seem to think it was funny at all. "Why in the world would you dream that?" I quickly added, realizing there must be a reason why she was sharing her dream with me.

"I really feel that God was letting me know you're supposed to marry Samuel," she answered.

Samuel, I thought—a little confused—why would I marry him? What about Gregario? I had always thought God would let me marry the one I loved… I can't marry Samuel, my heart whispered. I don't love him, I love Gregario!

Suddenly, I remembered the picture of Samuel standing by Amy's grave. Recalling the overwhelming feeling of empathy I had felt when I looked at his face, I also remembered the desire to ease his pain—a pain I felt so strongly that it hurt just to think about it… Maybe my desire to ease his suffering was God's way of telling me I was supposed to marry him, I thought… Then I envisioned Amy and her three children—knowing how happy she would be if I was part of their lives, loving them as she would have loved them. I even imagined her saying, "Will you do this for me, Vera?"

As strong waves of responsibility and the desire to honor my beautiful sister washed over me, I suddenly felt very afraid. Looking at my mom, I whispered, "I need to pray about this, Mom... I will marry him if it's what God is telling you I'm supposed to do—but, please, just let me pray about it first."

"Of course you can," she said, handing me the last piece of clothing to hang on the line. Then she said something that stayed with me for a very, very long time... "Make sure you don't pray for God to let you do what you want. Ask him to show you what he wants you to do. Follow God's voice, Vera—not your own."

Her words constantly echoed in my head, keeping me trapped in fear. *Follow God's voice and not your own,* for me, meant follow what your parents tell you to do—and disregard any feelings you have that go against it... Truth be known, I was quite good at disregarding my own feelings. I'd been practicing for a long time. Whenever I had a strong feeling in my heart, as though something were tugging at me—trying to get my attention—I just ignored it, telling myself it was the devil trying to get me to ignore God's wishes.

Why would I dare listen to myself? I'm just a girl put on this earth for men, I thought... Men and God—totally interchangeable, according to my father. I couldn't possibly know what would be best for me. I *did* believe in prayers though and normally I *did* ask God questions, but I didn't really believe God was going to give me any answers—especially about marrying Samuel.

It was obvious that Mom's mind was made up, and I was sure she had already told Dad. At least by asking to pray about it first, I had bought myself a little time to get used to the idea... I did, however, pray to God—asking him to bless me, and help me stifle the voice of my heart so I could get over Gregario and do what I was supposed to do. And, in some ways, I truly believed he did.

Later that day, Mom and Dad drove into town to purchase bus tickets to Chihuahua. Floyd and Dad were still very good friends, and he would be going back with Dad for a visit. Trying to recruit more followers, he often spent time in Chihuahua doing just that— believing every step of the way that my dad would eventually make up his mind to follow him too. After all, Dad did have one of his wives living amongst Floyd's followers, and he *had* managed to convince him a half-dozen times, although my father was known for swaying from follower to non-follower quite often. They both be- lieved in Jerome's teachings, but Dad continuously went back and forth between Floyd being, and not being, the next messenger—as he claimed he was.

They were gone for a few hours and when they returned, rain was pouring from the sky. I despised the rain in this part of Mexico. With no sidewalks for a clean landing, red, sticky mud ended up everywhere—even inside the house. One foot out the door would put you ankle deep in mud and trying to make it to and from the outhouse was a complete nightmare!

Mom and Dad sloshed through the mud and relentless rain into the house. This was the strongest rainfall I had ever witnessed, and I wondered if our home would sustain it. Just as I had that thought, our roof began to leak. Streams of water began running down the walls and puddles formed in the middle of the floor as rainwater dripped from out dilapidated ceiling. It was as if the heavens were crying! And, even though Mom put a few old buckets beneath the drips, they filled up faster than we could empty them.

I couldn't help but think of the huge mess I would have to clean up in the morning, especially when the kids began traipsing in and out. Most of the time all my cleaning and scrubbing was futile until things began to dry out a little, which sometimes took a few days. So, trying not to feel as gloomy as the weather, I spent a few mo- ments being thankful that I had gotten all the laundry done before the storm hit—and that Dad would be leaving tomorrow. I was tired of hearing about Jerome and his gospel and still had a hard time managing the fear I felt whenever my dad was around.

It was my silent joy to see his suitcase sitting open on Mom's bed... She was neatly folding and packing his clothes. But then I noticed her suitcase sitting next to his, and I wondered if she was going to Chihuahua with Dad and hadn't told me yet.

As if she could read my mind, Mom said, "Vera, that suitcase is for you. Your dad and I talked about you today and we both believe it will be good for you to go up to Chihuahua for a few months."

Excitement rocketed through me as I thought about seeing Gregario again. But just as quickly as it had come, I let it go—deliberately stopping myself from even thinking about him as I remembered Mom's dream.

"Becca will be going too," she added. "This is a perfect opportunity for you two girls to spend some time with your fathers. (Becca's dad was temporarily living in Chihuahua with one of his plural wives.)

I was excited about the idea of getting out of Quintana-roo and farther away from Wade, but I was also afraid of Mom's dream, knowing I would have to face Samuel in Chihuahua.

Mom handed me the suitcase and instructed me to start packing... As I went through my few belongings, deciding what to take and what to leave, I had a strong feeling that whatever I left behind I would never see again. A deep sadness filled my heart, which scared and confused me. In my hopes and dreams, I had always imagined myself leaving this Godforsaken place and reuniting with Gregario—but things were not happening the way I had planned. Wade was never part of my dream, and neither was Samuel. This must certainly be the cause of my sadness, I thought, wondering if I might be causing God to feel sad too. Maybe all the rain really was God crying for me, and my future. Maybe he already knew that it was going to be very different from what I had hoped or believed it would be.

I finished packing, then went to find Mom to see if she needed help with anything. Everyone was gathered around the table enjoying their supper together. I looked at each one of my siblings as I mentally expressed and silently sent my love to them. Although I was only going to Chihuahua for a few months something inside my heart told me that I would not be seeing them again for a very long time. Possibly years!

CHAPTER FOURTEEN

THIS I PRAY IN THE NAME OF YOUR SON, NOT YOUR DAUGHTER

I have heard that purifying your soul is like dipping a muddy cloth into fresh water a million times—then a million times more. Dipping, dipping, dipping until your soul is so clean and so pure you no longer recognize it as your own.

At five a.m., I awoke to the sound of Mom's soft voice. She would be driving us into town to catch the bus and was waking me to get ready… Rubbing my eyes, I grabbed the flashlight, preparing myself for the trek to the outhouse.

More asleep than awake and only two steps out the door, I slipped and fell into the mud. Not only was I sitting in it, but I was covered with it—from head to toe. Oh great, I thought—picking myself up and trying to shake the mud off my hands while my eyes combed the ground, desperately hoping my flashlight had landed somewhere near.

Mud-covered, but still shining a beam of light in the opposite direction, I bent down and picked it up, then managed my way through the mud to the water tap… This is *not* how I intended to start my day, I muttered to myself... I hated it. I hated red mud. I hated what it did outside and, even more, I hated what it did inside—turning a somewhat clean home into a pigsty. Furiously, I dug my fingernails into my skin, leaving echoes of claw marks on my arms and legs—rubbing and scrubbing till it hurt, hell-bent on ridding myself of it forever—almost as if I were washing away all that was, exposing the next layer of my life: the layer beneath the mud. The layer that was clean and pure—untouched and untarnished.

Finally semi-clean, I trudged off to the outhouse, then back home to get ready to leave; thoughts ricocheting through my head... What a disaster I was leaving behind—water and mud everywhere! I felt guilty that I wasn't going to be able to help Mom clean up the mess, and I wished she was leaving this place too. If only we could all move back to Chihuahua, I thought. If only.

Giving each of my siblings a goodbye hug, I held onto them a little longer than usual. I also held onto the hope that they, too, could leave this place someday—and that we'd all be together again.

When Becca and I had climbed into the back of the truck, Mom closed the camper, then hopped into the front seat between Dad and Floyd. As soon as she was settled, we made our way down the bumpy road, out of town, toward the highway.

The bed of the truck squeaked and rattled as I laid down on a blanket next to Becca, trying to process my feelings of excitement and sadness—coupled with fear and shame... Excited about a new journey, sad about leaving Mom and the kids behind, fear about my future, and shame when even a sliver of Wade wedged itself into my mind.

I looked over at Becca, whose long, brown hair framed her face. A dark mole on the side of her chin added a touch of sophisticated beauty to her square jaw, and her olive-colored skin was enough to make any girl jealous... She looked so at peace laying there with her eyes closed, and I wondered if she, too, felt the same way I felt—although I knew in my heart that she probably didn't.

She was one of four sisters, one born right after the other who shared in the chores at her house... You're so lucky, I thought. So lucky that your mom doesn't have only you to rely on. If I knew that my mom had someone to help her while I was away, I would not be feeling the way I'm feeling right now—but my little sister is still too young to help, and I'm worried about my mom having to do all the work by herself.

Realizing that Becca was sound asleep, I listened to her rhythmic breathing—the in-and-out journey of an invisible life force keeping even the seemingly worthless ones alive. The sound was so peaceful—obviously not caring who it kept alive—gently encouraging me to take a few deep breaths myself, relaxing into thoughts about Gregario... More than two years had passed since we'd seen each other, and I wondered if he had changed as much as I had... I strolled down memory lane, all the way back to the first time we'd met, then on to the square dances and the times we'd spent together swimming at his dad's farm; and, of course, to the love notes. Oh, those love notes—how they made me smile! But what I remembered most was how I felt when I was around him—like a princess who was adored by a prince. And through all the sadness and the guilt and the shame, I felt excited about seeing him again—even though I knew I could not marry him. Mom's dream had been on my mind a lot, and I had started to believe that Samuel was the man I was supposed to marry. I would become his third wife and would be living celestial marriage—the only key to access the full range of God's kingdom.

We arrived at the bus depot and after loading our suitcases, I hugged Mom goodbye. It was so hard to let her go and I tried my best not to cry as I boarded the bus.

I sat next to Dad, feeling a little apprehensive about being so close to him in such a small space for such a long time. He slept a lot during the ride, and I caught myself staring at him...

As I watched him sleeping, I wondered who my father really was—then finally came up with this: He is my dad, the man my mom is in love with. The man who is going to take her to Heaven with him.

I leaned in a little closer and continued to stare. His head was tilted back, his jaw was loosened and in his relaxed state, the wrinkles on his forehead didn't look quite as deep as they usually did. For a moment he didn't seem so scary to me—he just looked like a normal dad taking a nap.

My eyes still glued to the man who ruled my life, I asked myself why I was so afraid of him—but I couldn't come up with an answer. All I knew was that he made me feel unworthy, wicked, ashamed, and disgraceful. That little voice inside my heart—the one I always ignored—had tried to get me to believe that I couldn't possibly be those things, but I could not afford to listen and take the risk of being wrong. My eternal life depended on me paying close attention to Dad which, in my world, was equivalent to paying close attention to God—because in my world they were the same. The only difference was that God wore flowing white robes and had white hair and a beard, and my dad looked more like a cowboy. But inside my head, I see them as one even though my heart keeps insisting that one is human, and the other is not.

As I continued watching Dad sleep, the bus driver drove us farther away from Quintana-roo *and* from Mom—reminding me of how much I missed her already. Focused on my memories of her beautiful smile, her warm hugs, and her soft, loving words, I suddenly realized that when I think of her, I don't ever picture God.

I'd never been taught about a motherly God and I tried to remember a time when I may have been told about a Heavenly Mother... My mind raced back to Sunday school, prayer meetings and anywhere else I may have been taught about her. But I couldn't recall a single biblical story about a divine, precious mother. All the stories had been about God the Father, not God the Mother.

A feeling of unworthiness washed over me as I concluded that women must not matter to God—because, after all, he never even mentions them in the Bible. I pondered this for a while, thinking that it might be why God never speaks about his own wife, or perhaps that should be 'wives.' Plural as opposed to just one.

Still struggling to accept the fact that I'm only here on earth to serve a man, I returned to my memories of Mom and all the kindness and love I feel when I'm around her. A part of me wants to argue with God that it's not fair that he doesn't care about his daughters like he does about his sons... *Look at all Mom is,* I silently said to God, imagining myself wrapping my arms around her, whispering, "I've got you, Mom. I love you and I think you are way better than Dad—even if God doesn't see it."

I desperately wanted to tell God he was wrong, but I knew I shouldn't be feeling what I was feeling—and, suddenly, filled with shame for questioning what I had always been taught, I closed my eyes, bowed my head, and offered God a prayer:

> *Please forgive me, Heavenly Father, for allowing these evil thoughts to come into my mind. I will try harder to understand your ways even if they don't make sense, and I won't ask about my heavenly mother again. I'm sorry. This I pray in the name of your Son, not your daughter... Amen.*

Opening my eyes, I looked at Dad again—still sleeping. I hoped that God, too, was taking a nap—because, although I had tried to be sincere with my prayer, I was still angry about the unfairness of boys becoming kings and girls becoming slaves. And, if God was sleeping, perhaps he would not be able to feel my anger.

As if my silent conversation with God had disturbed his sleep, Dad stirred. Yawning, he opened his eyes and straightened up.

"Boy, was I tired," he said, raising his arms above his head and stretching.

Nervously, I looked away, not wanting him to know what I had been thinking about while he slept. I leaned my head back on the seat, closed my eyes, and hoped he would think I had fallen asleep... I just couldn't listen to any of his preaching right now, especially one of his rampages about the goodness of God. I was struggling to get past my angry feelings, and I knew if Dad said anything about the God he worshiped with every fiber of his being, I would burst into tears and would have to tell him why I was crying. I didn't want to share how degrading it is to be a girl, or how sad I felt whenever I remembered that Mom and I were nothing more than helpmates for men. How would I ever explain how unfair I often think God is? So, I didn't dare put myself in a position where I might have to tell him how I *really* felt and kept my eyes closed—pretending to be asleep.

"Vera, you sleeping?" I heard him say, opening my eyes and sheepishly looking over at him.

"No," I answered. "I'm just resting my eyes."

He looked closely at me, and in a serious tone, he said, "Your mother told me about her dream. I think it's important that you pay attention to what she told you. God works in mysterious ways and I don't think it's a coincidence that your mother had the dream right after Samuel's attempt to come and see you."

"Was Samuel the man you were talking about when you said a Saunders boy was coming down to see me?" I asked—a knot starting to form in my stomach... Twisting itself into a tangle and getting tighter and tighter, the knot made me wince with the realization that this was yet another sign from God. A sign that I was supposed to marry Amy's husband, Samuel—my brother-in-law.

"Yes," he replied. "He's a big talker like his mother, but aside from that he's a good, God-fearing man. Your sister loved him very much, and it saddens me that he doesn't have her anymore. So, if he chooses to marry you, you should count your blessings, Vera."

I sat there, listening to what he was saying—wanting to ask him questions about marrying someone. The words "your sister loved him very much" echoed through my mind and I was plagued with the thought that if she got to marry the man she loved, why did I not get to marry a man I loved? Does love only matter in celestial marriage if you're the first wife? Amy had been a first wife and Mama Vee was a first wife—and they were both very much in love with the men they married.

I wondered if it was fair to marry Samuel even though I didn't love him, then mustered up the courage to ask, "What if I can't ever fall in love with him, Dad? Would God still want me to marry him?"

"What kind of question is that?" he asked, looking at me as though I had lost my mind. "Love is a decision, not a feeling. You can decide who you want to fall in love with the minute you make up your mind about it, and you better decide to love Samuel if God's will is that you marry him."

His words knocked me right off the high-flying "love is a feeling" horse I had been riding... Love is a decision? If that was true, then not to love must also be a decision... So, do I just decide not to love Gregario anymore, and decide to love Samuel?

Once again, the need to deny my own feelings in order to go along with what my parents believed was "God's will," sent my heart into a locked chamber. A chamber where it would not be heard, no matter how loud it screamed... I trusted Mom and her dream, and by trusting what Dad had just said I started to believe that perhaps I could do it—perhaps I *could* marry Samuel, even if I really didn't want to. After all, I had prayed for God to bless me and help me get over Gregario. And maybe this was that blessing.

CHAPTER FIFTEEN

MEETING THE WHITE BIRD

Sometimes, the only way to survive reality is to fly above it in your mind—to create a new world in the sky, a world where you are free. And, although imagining your way there may not change the reality you eventually return to, it does—eventually—change the person who is returning.

After two-and-a-half days of bus rides, we finally arrived in Chihuahua at noon on Saturday—in the middle of April. The sun was shining brightly, matching my somewhat lighter spirit. I was excited to be back, to see all the family, and somewhere in my soul I felt strength, believing that I would be able to handle whatever was in store for me.

Despite the new roads and homes that had been built since I'd left, much of it remained the same—although I was not the same girl who had left there. So, maybe these were my new roads, I thought hopefully, and maybe they would take me somewhere wonderful—a place where my heart would be happy. Although, at this point, true happiness was hard to imagine, but I tried.

Dad had agreed to let me stay with my older sister, Cheryl, as long as I checked in with him and Mama Vee every day; and just the thought of staying with my sister instead of with Dad lifted my heart—no sermons, no inner-turmoil, no frightening thoughts of burning in hell. Just my sister's smiling face and warm hugs.

Cheryl's husband had just built her (and her sister wife) a new home. It was big and spacious, and I would have a bedroom all to myself. I'd always had a good relationship with her and felt completely comfortable knowing that I'd be staying with her.

After arriving at her home and meeting her sister wife and all the children, I'm sure she sensed how much I had missed everyone and how good it felt to be surrounded by my family again, so she suggested we drive to Aunt Sally's house to visit for the afternoon...

Aunt Sally—genuinely happy to see me—welcomed me with a warm hug, then asked how my mother was doing.

"She's fine," I said—remembering the muddy house, my younger siblings, and the mother I had left behind—hoping my words were true and that she really was fine.

"I sure miss her and wish your dad would bring her back here to live... You know he had your brother, Jake, build her a home over by where Samuel's two houses are, right?"

"No, I didn't know," I answered—wondering why he would leave Mom in mud-town when she could be living here in a nice house, safe from deadly things that slithered in the night and vicious plants that made you wish you were never born... Why? Why would he leave her there all by herself to raise a houseful of young children—desperately trying to make ends meet as her feet sank into the mud?

"Yeah," continued Aunt Sally, "we all heard that he was bringing her back but for some reason he never did, and now Jake has moved his first wife into the home that was built for your mom.

Trying not to let it show, a disgusted feeling came over me... Dad's decision to build Mom a house here must have been made in a period of doubt, I thought, but I guess he changed his mind. He was forever questioning whether Floyd was really who he claimed to be, and because he could never make up his mind and stick with it, the one who suffered most was my mother.

Later that evening, back at Cheryl's—after helping her put her children to bed—we stayed up talking for hours. We talked about Mom, our siblings, and all the latest community news. We also talked about marriage, and she said she had a favor to ask of me.

"Of all the men that you could pay attention to while you're here, please pay attention to Samuel. I've felt so bad for him since Amy's death—he seems so sad—and even though he has a second wife, Stella, she isn't a very good wife to him. But you would be a good wife for him," she said, laughing a little, as though she felt embarrassed. "Besides, it would make us double related. Not only are we sisters, we would be sisters-in-law as well!"

Cheryl's husband and Samuel were brothers, which was probably why she was so concerned about him, but her words only reminded me of Mom's dream and my impossibly possible future. So, trying to stay as far away from the subject of Samuel as possible, I asked her about Gregario. To which she replied, "He's been out of town for a long time now, working in the States." Then immediately went back to talking about Samuel—telling me that he was planning on attending tomorrow's Sunday class, which was being held in her home. Just the thought of coming face-to-face with him filled me with dread—until she mentioned that his children would probably be coming with him. It was a tiny light in the darkness of my soul... I loved my sister's children and, even if it meant seeing Samuel too, I couldn't wait to wrap my arms around them.

In all the times I had seen him before, it had never crossed my mind that one day Samuel might be my husband. And, somehow, the thought of marrying him didn't seem right. Amy had loved him; I did not—but then again, I did love his children. They were my sister's children—the children she had brought into this world; the children she had adored.

Waking up the next morning, I was a little confused about where I was when I first opened my eyes—then, breathing in the fresh scent of clean sheets, I suddenly remembered that I was in Chihuahua at Cheryl's house—and that the Sunday meeting would probably be starting soon. I had no idea what time it was, but I jumped out of bed searching for my suitcase, which I finally found in the bedroom across the hall. Glancing at the clock, I realized I only had a few minutes to get ready to meet both what I dreaded and what I loved.

Quickly showering and dressing, the smell of toast drew me into the kitchen, and I hoped I would have enough time to eat before the meeting started. But the minutes were quickly disappearing, and I knew I would be coming face-to-face with Samuel soon, so—filled with fear at the thought of seeing him, as well as excitement about seeing his children—I slipped back into the bedroom to say a quick prayer. Needing to calm my nerves, I wanted to ask God to please make me like Samuel if marrying him is what he wanted me to do.

From the hallway, I suddenly heard a man's voice—Samuel—asking Cheryl where I was; saying that he thought I was going to be here. Then I heard her tell him that I was here, which jolted me out of prayer and into action. I knew I needed to go out and join the others, so I made my way down the hall toward the front room—on my way to the man I was supposed to marry.

Samuel watched me walk into the room. He was sitting on the couch with Amy's three children—along with a few others who had come for the Sunday class. I didn't see Stella anywhere, so I nervously made eye contact with him as he stood up to shake my hand—putting his other arm around my shoulders as he did. Shaking in my shoes, I greeted him politely, then leaned down to hug the children.

"That's your Mom's sister," Samuel said to them. "Give her a hug."

Excited to meet me, all three of them wrapped their arms around me and hugged me tight. A strong wave of emotion washed over me. I had waited for this moment and these hugs for so long and now that they were happening, I never wanted them to stop. I held each child, taking my time and making sure they could feel my love before letting them go... They were three precious angels—and a feeling of wanting to protect them welled up inside me. I knew I could not replace their mother, but I could shower them with love as she would have. And I wanted to—with all my heart, I wanted to.

Andrew, the oldest, who looked a lot like his dad, held onto me the longest. As I let him go, he looked deep into my eyes as though he were looking for something, then he smiled and hugged me again. I could sense his longing for his mom—and I could also sense his connection with me, the person who was, and always would be, connected to his mother.

I sat on the couch across from Samuel and his kids during the class. Elise, the youngest daughter, kept running over to me and sitting on my lap. She was bubbly and energetic and couldn't sit still, going back and forth between her dad's lap and mine as though it were a fun game.

Alice, the middle child, was much calmer. She kept her little arms folded and tried paying attention to the class like her big brother. She came and sat next to me for a little while during the class, holding my hand as she played with my fingers. When she looked up at me, smiling, a little knot formed in the back of my throat. I tried not to cry as I recognized the smile. It was identical to Amy's. She looked so much like her, with thick blonde hair and sparkling green eyes—catapulting me into so many memories of the sister I missed with all my heart.

When the class was over, Samuel—getting ready to leave, picked up Elise, then looked at me, saying, "It was nice to see you again. How long are you here for?"

"For a couple of months—maybe," I said nervously, hoping my anxiety wasn't obvious.

Although I wanted the children to stay, I couldn't wait for him to leave. Something about him made me feel apprehensive and later, when Cheryl asked me how things went, I bravely told her the truth, "He seems nice, but I get a strange, hyper-nervous feeling from him." Or maybe, I thought, it could be that I'm just nervous myself, haunted by Mom's dream.

"Yes," said Cheryl, "he's very high strung with a lot of nervous energy—which is why he always talks so much. Everyone in town calls him 'the talker' but if you can look past that, you'll see that he's a good man."

I remembered Dad's words and how he had said almost the exact same thing about Samuel. They were both politely letting me know he had a weakness for gossip—but that it was harmless, and I could easily overlook it—which I did. But, one day—in the not-too-far-away-future, I would find out just how detrimental to the success of celestial marriage this weakness really was.

Later in the day, I slipped back into the bedroom to take a nap. The late night with Cheryl, along with the long trip, had gotten the best of me and I just could not keep my eyes open. Laying down on the bed, thinking I would fall asleep as soon as my head hit the pillow—I suddenly saw flashes of Amy, Samuel and their three children... Thoughts about celestial marriage and my desire to make it to Heaven screeched through my mind, sending me into a state of utter despair—and the only way to turn it off was to surrender to my imagination.

I took a few deep breaths and saw myself in a new world where everything I could ever want was before me. I was no longer a confused, frightened girl walking around in broken shoes and torn clothes, desperately seeking an identity. I imagined myself attending school, studying to become a doctor... Now I'm popular, I thought. I have lots of friends who love me even though I'm a bit prissy and wear the most expensive clothes I can find. When I speak, my friends listen to me, and they care about what I have to say... Nobody seems worried about making it to Heaven because they all know they are naturally going to end up there, no matter what they've been taught to believe... I'm having fun while I'm learning about medicine. I love people and the idea of saving lives makes me happy. I know someday I will marry a man who loves me, but there's no hurry—this is my time to just learn and discover and have fun... I'm rich and pretty but the most important thing is that I am free. I am free to express my feelings. My own feelings, the ones that mean so much to me—the ones God never heard because I hid them from him. The feelings I've learned to ignore, suddenly, in this world—my new world—I am able to express. And I feel so alive! So free to be me!

I think I must be really dreaming now, I mumbled silently, because I have wings. Big, white and blue wings, and I'm soaring. I'm a bird and I can fly anywhere. I'm free to fly, to be, and to feel! Somewhere in the big, endless sky, as I'm flying through the clouds, there is a God who is flying with me. A God I know loves me. A God that values my freedom as much as I do.

CHAPTER SIXTEEN

FEELINGS OF THE SOUL

My own secrets became ghosts—ghosts with wings. And I kept them hidden because at the time I didn't know that ghosts with wings are really angels. And that angels don't stay hidden for very long.

The following day, meeting up with Bonita, we decided to ask Mr. Shields—a polygamist member of the church—if we could ride his horses. They were being kept in Samuel's backyard corral, and we wanted to ride around town and say hello to all of Dad's family.

Bonita's house was on Dad's lot—right across the road from Samuel's two houses, built side by side, one bigger than the other, facing the same road. The bigger home was built for Amy—who had been his first wife—to accommodate her growing family. Stella, his second wife, had not had any children yet, and the smaller home was built for her. After Amy died, Stella moved into the big house and Amy's three children lived with her—leaving the smaller house available for Samuel's next wife, whom he hadn't chosen yet, so he had loaned it to his sister. Both homes shared the same backyard which had a big barn, a tool shed and corrals for goats and horses.

Samuel loved goats and had three or four thoroughbred milking goats which supplied him and his family with plenty of milk for most of the year. He also had horses and was the only one around who knew what Bonita and I needed to know—how to saddle a horse. And even though neither of us wanted to ask him for help, we really did want to ride through town, so it was either ask him or don't go.

Bonita begged me to be the one to ask. She said there was something about Samuel that made her feel embarrassed, which definitely got my attention, so I asked her what she meant by "something."

"Let's just say that I can tell he likes me," she said. "But I don't like him at all, and I don't want to take the chance of him possibly thinking that I do."

Well, I'm not interested in him either, I thought, but obviously I don't get to choose like you do because God never sent your mom a dream about you marrying him. Quickly putting that thought aside, I walked across the road to Samuel's backyard knowing that I needed to get used to talking to him sometime, deciding that it might as well be now.

Standing near the corral in his backyard, I suddenly and desperately hoped he wasn't home. The voice of dread rang in my ears, but before I could turn around and flee, I saw him come out of the well-house and set the muddy bucket and rope he was carrying on the ground. Bracing myself, I watched him walk toward me. Wearing a baggie T-shirt, baggy jeans, a cap, and rubber boots—covered in mud from head to toe—he stood in front of me and, obviously embarrassed about the state of his clothes, he explained that he had been digging a well.

For some reason, I found myself feeling sorry for him and truly wanted to ease his embarrassment—but I didn't say anything. Instead, I just watched him wash his hands under the nearby tap.

When he was done and had dried his hands with a dirty rag, he extended his hand to me, saying, "I'm too dirty or else I'd hug you."

Shaking his hand, I pretended to be calm—which I was not, but at least I was trying.

Eyeing the bridle I was holding, he asked if I needed help with something.

"Yes," I answered, somewhat bravely, "Mr. Shields said Bonita and I could borrow his horses, and I was wondering if you could help us gear them up? I don't know how to do it myself, otherwise I wouldn't bother you."

"It's no problem," he said. "I'd be glad to help."

As he saddled up the horses, that strong feeling of empathy returned. It was scary and confusing—probably, I decided, because I know how much Amy loved him. The way her eyes used to light up every time she talked about him. Even when she spoke about him marrying Stella, her eyes lit up. As I did, she strongly believed in celestial marriage and she stayed faithful and strong when he took a second wife—gracefully stepping into the covenant of celestial marriage right along with him.

Another wave of empathy rushed through me as he handed me the reins. "Here you go," he said politely—and then came another wave.

Thanking him, I led the horses across the street—back to Bonnie's house. I couldn't understand why the thought of him suffering, or even being uncomfortable, made me feel so bad when I didn't even like him. Maybe these feelings are God's way of making me like him enough to marry him, I thought. That must be what they are. And I must listen to God. I must do whatever he wants me to do, even when it's hard.

After riding around town for a few hours, then returning Mr. Shields' horses, I noticed Samuel's mother hanging clothes outside on the line. Stopping to say hello to her, she seemed eager to talk to me—taking great pleasure in humorously teasing me about marrying one of her sons. "Samuel would sure like to marry another one of your father's daughters," she said light-heartedly. "Maybe you'll get to be the lucky one!"

Not daring to mention my mom's dream, I made every effort to laugh with her—even though I knew she was much more serious about me marrying her son than she let on... I was barely sixteen but considered plenty old enough to be married. And it seemed that wherever I went or whoever I spoke to, everyone wanted to pair me up with the nearest available polygamist. And, of course, there were many who were available because there was no limit to how many wives they could have—and age difference was of no concern to any of them. Most of them were much older than I was—ranging in age from thirty to fifty-something—and Samuel was one of them. Not that he was a nasty old man like some of them were, but just the thought of him touching me made my entire body cringe, and his mother's comments certainly didn't help any—so, starting to feel sick to my stomach, I quickly said goodbye.

Walking back to Cheryl's house, my thoughts continued to spin out of control... I know I've grown up over the years—that I'm changing from a girl into a woman—but until recently I didn't realize that my now well-developed breasts meant that I was going to be hung on display in a meat market, a meat market where the majority of shoppers are older, married men. It sickens me just to think about it, but what am I to do? Yes, I feel sorry for Samuel. And, yes, his suffering makes me want to curl up and cry. And, yes, I know how much he loved my sister, Amy. I definitely understand his pain. I miss her too. I weep for her too. And my heart aches whenever I think about her too. And, yes, I would like to offer him some comfort—knowing that his heart is filled with grief. There is no way I could not know it—not feel it—because being loved by Amy was like being loved by an angel; and that kind of love is incredibly hard to let go of. But marry him? Now there's a whole new twist on compassion… I need to pray, I thought. I need to pray hard. I need to tell God I'm sorry. And then I need to pray even harder.

A few days later, I walked into Mama Vee's house to do my daily check-in with Dad but was blindsided by what greeted me. There was Samuel, sitting on the couch with Dad and Mama Vee. Nearly swallowing my own tongue, I managed a weak, "Hello." Then stood there rattled to the core.

"We were just talking about you," said Dad, "and wondering when you were going to show up. Samuel needs a babysitter for his children today, but we can't babysit because we're going out for a while. So we volunteered you if that's all right."

"That's perfectly all right with me," I said—feeling a little calmer and thanking God that his only mission was to find a babysitter.

Samuel smiled as his two little girls came into the front room, and suddenly everything changed… I couldn't help but feel excited, and I was genuinely happy about spending time with them—but I noticed that his son was missing and wondered where he was.

As if he could read my mind, Samuel said, "My son is at a friend's house and won't be coming. I only need you to keep an eye on the girls if you don't mind."

"I don't mind," I said, as my sister's beautiful little girls hugged me

Shortly after Samuel left, Dad and Mama Vee left as well… I sat on the floor and pulled out a few children's books from the shelf next to the basket of toys Mama Vee kept for the grandkids. I asked both girls which one they wanted me to read to them. Alice immediately chose the one with a puppy on it but Elise wasn't interested at all. Her little hand grasping a flyswatter, she hit me across the face with it, then hollered, "Be good or I'm going to whip you!"

I couldn't help but laugh at my feisty three-year-old niece—guessing that she was probably playing a mimicking game of some sort. Reaching out and trying to take the flyswatter away, I was a little surprised when she pulled her tiny arm back and hollered again, "You be good, you be good!"

Standing up, I took the flyswatter out of her hand, saying, "Come on, sweetheart, let's read a book with Aunt Vera."

She immediately threw herself on the floor and began kicking and screaming while hollering, "Give it to me, give it to me!" Then she began to cry as if the world had just ended for her.

Determined to win her over, I picked her up off the floor—still kicking and screaming—rocked her in my arms and began singing... Alice sat on the floor leafing through the books, patiently waiting for me to start reading, and it wasn't long before Elise stopped crying and laid quietly in my arms staring up at me. I continued to sing to her as I brushed her hair away from her face and wiped the tears from her eyes. She looked at Alice, then back at me and said, "Book."

"You want me to read to you now?" I asked gently.

She nodded her head, so I sat on the floor once again and began to read the puppy book to both of them—making barking sounds and animal noises. They were delighted, and they laughed and giggled while I read. Later, I gave them cookies and played with them until Mama Vee got home.

Something beautiful had happened during the time we spent together... Not only did I fall deeper in love with the girls, which was so easy for me to do, but I sensed Amy's love was with us too. I could feel her presence, and I believed the girls felt it too. How lucky I was to be part of their lives—two precious souls, missing their mother, but allowing me to share the love that Amy would have shared with them if she could have.

Three weeks after arriving in Chihuahua, as I was returning to Cheryl's house after being out for a while, I noticed a bike leaning against her front porch. And, as I walked into the living room, I was only mildly surprised when Samuel stood up, smiled at me, and said hello.

"Can I talk to you for a few minutes?" he asked, replacing his smile with a rather serious look.

From the way he spoke I knew that what he had to say must be important to him, but was it going to be important to me? Strangely enough, I already knew the answer to that question and, once again, my nerves began to tremble, knowing exactly what was coming.

"What is it, Samuel?" I asked, as calmly as I could—pretending to be tired, sinking down on the couch and putting one arm over my face as a way to stop my eyes from revealing the truth of my feelings.

Sitting down next to me, I could feel his words coming before he even said them, and I knew that after this talk, my life would never be the same again… He reached for my hand, then sat quietly for a minute—as if he didn't know how to say what he wanted to say.

I already know that I am to marry you, I thought—so can we hurry up and get this part over with? I am tired of the dread I've been feeling.

Again, as though he could read my mind, he said, "I would like to have your permission to court you and would love for you to join my family."

A part of me wanted to say, *No, I don't want to court you! No, I don't want to be part of your family! No, I don't want to marry you,* but how could I possibly say no to him? I believed I had no other option and if I said no to him, I would be saying no to God—which would mean no Heaven for me.

Suddenly, he reached for the hand covering my face and moved it away, saying, "Let me look into your beautiful eyes."

You have never even seen my eyes, I thought—looking away. And I don't want you looking into them. You scare me. You scare the hell out of me. But, suddenly—just like a robot—I heard myself say, "If my dad gives you permission to marry me, then I will."

And, of course, my dad was going to give his permission. I knew it and he knew it. My mom knew it and his mom knew it, too. The whole world probably knew it... My heart shuttered, just like the leaves on the trees shutter in the fall, right before they drop and die. Then a great wind sweeps through the valley, and they disappear. Without ever actually saying the word "yes," I had sealed the deal—the deal that I had made with God to submit and obey. Now, it would only be a matter of time before I was married off to my deceased sister's husband.

With a faraway look in his eyes, Samuel smiled—and, suddenly, sure that he was probably thinking of Amy, I thought of her too. And her children. And their need for my love. And how much I really did want to love them. And how much I was counting on their love to help me survive this marriage—this celestial marriage—to their father. This marriage that is God and the prophet's written-in-stone law.

As Samuel stood up to leave, he wrapped his arms around me, hugging me before walking out the door. Watching him through the window, with no one else home to hear, I screamed out loud, "No!"

I had a horrible sinking feeling in my stomach. A dark and dreary feeling coupled with pain. It felt like death. It felt like and empty branch crying out—trying to save its own leaves. All I wanted to do was run after Samuel and tell him the truth. That I can't do it. That marrying him feels very, very wrong to me. But when I looked out the window again, I saw the father of my sister's precious children riding away—looking happy and excited. A happy and excited that I just could not take away from him. Or my father. Or God.

Frantically, I ran down the hallway, locked myself in the bedroom, and fell to my knees—begging and pleading for God's understanding... "I know I said I would do this," I cried, "and I'm sorry for being so weak-minded. I just don't know what to do with all these feelings, God. I really don't want to marry him. I don't even know him and all that he knows about me is that I am Amy's half-sister. Even if I do this for her children, what should I do about my feelings? Can I please not do this and still have your love? Please... I will still be there for Amy's children, I promise!"

I continued to plead with God but received no relief. It was useless, and I felt myself letting go, surrendering to my lot in life—quickly changing my prayer to one of obedience.

"Okay, God," I said, as I went from kneeling down to laying on the floor. My eyes were feeling sore and swollen but the tears had finally stopped. "I will make you proud and show you that I can set a good example of celestial marriage by being a good wife and sister wife. I'll learn to keep the feelings I struggle with buried, the same way we bury someone who has died."

Exhausted, I gave in to the laws of my Father—truly believing that I needed to let my own feelings die in order for God's will to live.

CHAPTER SEVENTEEN

THE HEAVENLY GOAL

I had always thought of Heaven as a light and airy place.
But as soon as I claimed it, held it in my arms and walked
with it for a while, I realized how heavy Heaven was.

September 17, 1988 was the date set for our wedding. I had spent a
lot of time with Amy's children and had grown to love them even
more. However, Samuel's second wife, Stella, was a different story—and she made it very clear that she didn't like me. Although she
had married Samuel as a second wife herself, she was not happy
about him marrying me. And, unlike Amy, who had received her
with open arms and welcomed her into her family, Stella went out
of her way to let me know that she did not want to live by the laws
of celestial marriage now that Amy had died—and that she was only
going along with it because she loved Samuel but wasn't about to
give him up to any woman, much less me.

I couldn't imagine why he would have ever chosen her as his
second wife—she was crass, often heartless, always belligerent, and
about as far away from loving as a person could get. Knowing what
a kind and loving person Amy was, it seemed strange that he would
pick a second wife who was so different. At the time he was married to an angel, and it just didn't make sense that he would bring

someone like Stella into their family. But he had. And now it was my turn to deal with it.

Until she became my ever-present reality, I didn't realize she had never really believed in celestial marriage, like Amy and I did. But I trusted Samuel when he told me that she was only jealous because it was new. "She'll come around," he promised, whenever she threw a fit about something. "Don't let her scare you away, it really will get better."

Well, I was used to hoping for things, so I too held onto the belief that it would get better. I thought perhaps that after I married him, and she had gotten used to me, I could easily win her heart over—but was I ever wrong!

I had not seen Mom or the kids since leaving Quintana-roo a few months ago, and what saved me from completely falling apart was knowing that they would be at my wedding—which was only a few weeks away... Samuel was showing some interest in Floyd's doctrine, so he made a trip to Quintana-roo to see him—taking Stella along. Supposedly, he took her with him so they could spend some time alone before stepping back into the covenant of celestial marriage. Who knows? Maybe he took her with him so she wouldn't tie me up and toss me into the river! In which case, I probably should have been thankful. But right before our wedding, seemed like an odd time to take Stella on a honeymoon; although, most disconcerting of all, was that while they were in Quintana-roo to see Floyd, they also stopped in to visit all the family members who were currently living there, including Alondra and her husband, Wade.

On the evening of his return, he stopped at Cheryl's house to see me for a few minutes—handing me a letter from Mom after he hugged me. I still wasn't used to his hugs, and whenever I started to feel uncomfortable, I practiced a new disconnecting technique I had learned. It consisted of deep breaths along with exaggerated images of Heaven. It helped me stay focused on the goal—the heavenly goal... And this time, holding me a little longer than usual, I was completely surprised when, without warning, he suddenly kissed my mouth. Caught off guard because it happened so quickly, I didn't even have a chance to process what had just happened, when he suddenly kissed me again—longer this time, as I kept my lips tightly closed. This was nothing like I had imagined a kiss would be, but of course I had imagined my kisses to be with Gregario.

I don't like this, I thought, as he let go of me, saying, "I sure love ya."

I was incredibly uncomfortable, so I tried focusing on my breathing again while staring at the wall behind him.

"Well, aren't you going to say it back to me?" he asked.

Say it back to him, Vera, I told myself. Say it back! That's what people say to each other when they're going to be married. But I couldn't, and the silence felt impossibly awkward as he stood there, waiting for me to say something.

I had gotten used to the fact that I was going to marry him, but I still didn't know how to make myself love him. And, hard as I tried, I couldn't say anything.

Finally realizing that I wasn't going to say it back, he pulled me to him and hugged me again before asking, "Have you ever been kissed before?"

His question sent a nerve-wracking chill down my spine. I didn't want to lie to him but neither did I want to tell him the truth—if there even was a truth about the stranger with the apples and Wade. So, hesitantly, I somehow managed to whisper, "Sorta."

He held me away from him, gazing at my face. "What do you mean by sorta?" he asked suspiciously, as if my one-word answer was an admission of doing something wrong. "Either you have, or you haven't," he said, staring at me.

I knew that if I wasn't a virgin, I would have to tell him about Wade. But if I was still pure, I would never have to talk about him to anyone. But in a million years, I never expected to be asked about being kissed, and I wasn't quite sure how to respond; although, I was well aware that I had to tell the truth—well, some of it.

"I didn't willfully kiss anyone," I said, still staring at the wall behind him. "Alondra's husband, Wade, asked me to marry him and after I refused, he kissed me."

Perhaps sounding brave but secretly mortified, I went on to describe (as vaguely as possible) what Wade had done to me... The shame I felt when I told him that I didn't know if I was a virgin anymore made me want to run and hide—throw myself into a dark corner where the valueless people hang onto one another while they slowly die.

But, surprisingly calm, Samuel simply asked me for more details—more than I ever wanted to give anyone—then said, "From what you have described to me you are still a virgin, unless you passed out and don't remember everything that happened."

I reassured him that I did not pass out, and that I remembered it all.

"Then you're still a virgin," he said, confidently. "Don't worry about it."

I sighed in relief. The terrible burden I had been carrying around had finally been released, and I almost felt like I was indebted to him for relieving it—as though he had done something holy that allowed me to feel the worthiness of virginity again.

"Now it makes sense," he added, slightly nodding his head.

"What makes sense?" I asked, wondering what he meant.

"It makes sense that when I was visiting your sister and Wade and told them I was going to be marrying you, they both acted very strange. I didn't understand it at the time, but now it makes sense."

Not wanting to talk about it anymore, I didn't respond. And after a few quiet minutes passed, he said he should be going. "Stella probably has supper ready for me," he said, "and she'll be extremely upset if I'm here with you and not at home with her." Then he hugged me again saying "good night," and headed for the door.

Feeling nervous again after he left—and hoping he wouldn't share my secret with anyone—I sat on the edge of the bed and opened Mom's letter. A feeling of warmth immediately flowed through me as I looked at the familiar handwriting. Oh, how I longed to see her! She wrote that the kids had been asking when I would be coming home, and that she'd finally told them that I was getting married and was not coming back. They miss you so much, she wrote, which very nearly sent me into a torrent of tears.

I miss them too, I thought. I guess I never stopped to think about how hard it must have been on them for me to leave for a few weeks—then never come home. Trying to soften the sadness that was filling my heart, I remembered what Samuel had told me once, when I told him how homesick I often felt and how much I missed Mom. "The Bible says that a woman will cleave unto her husband," he had said. "That means that you will leave your family and friends and do whatever it takes to follow your husband."

Although he wasn't really my husband yet, I understood what he meant, and I told myself over and over again to toughen up.

It was the day before my wedding and, up until now, I had done exceedingly well when it came to remaining disconnected from my feelings. My sole focus was on nurturing Amy's children, which brought me tremendous joy. And, by now, I had convinced myself that the empathy I felt for Samuel was surely some sort of love—believing that Dad had been right: Loving someone was a decision.

Although I was only a child, believing that I was doing the right thing made me feel like a woman serving a master in order to serve God. And I discovered that the more I believed this holy doctrine of polygamy, the easier it got for me to move forward into a marriage that was my only ticket to Heaven.

Mom had arrived from Quintana-roo for the wedding with one of my younger brothers. She could not afford to bring all the kids, which was disappointing—but I knew she would have brought them all if she could have. And just seeing her again, made my heart dance.

Grandma too, traveled a great distance—coming all the way from Odessa to be here for the wedding; and I knew she had come simply to support me.

"She would not have traveled all this way if you were not special to her, Vera," Mom said. "We all want you to know how much we love you. Celestial marriage is a sacred covenant and we sure admire you for taking this step."

It was wonderful seeing Mom again, but it didn't satisfy the longing for her that I felt in my heart. I wanted to talk to her and tell her how I was really feeling. I wanted her to know I was afraid and that I felt as though a part of me was dying. I desperately wanted her to understand me, but I knew she couldn't. She was willfully blinded from the truth and believed that this was God's will for me. Even if my heart was suffering, it was God's will. And, of course she believed it—if she did not, how could she ever justify her own miserable existence?

As the day progressed, I began having more and more trouble disconnecting from my feelings the way I normally did. It was like getting so close to the fire that you couldn't help but feel the heat. A tightening started in the pit of my stomach and worked its way up into my chest, then my back. It felt like I was suffocating and although I tried to practice my breathing technique, it became increasingly harder to breathe as the moments ticked by.

I could feel myself breaking into a sweat, and my only thought was that I was going to die... Who cares if you die? I heard myself saying. Go ahead and die, it might just be easier for you! Which, believe it or not, actually made me feel better because at least it was my own voice and not someone else's.

My wedding night—just the thought of it—was terrifying... The idea of Samuel owning my life, my soul, and my body for his own pleasure, was not only scary, it was humiliating. I was sixteen years old; a child pretending to be a woman. A woman pretending to be a servant of God. A servant of God pretending to love a man who, according to the laws of polygamy, would soon become my master.

It was all so enormous, but I did find that keeping busy helped a little. And so I cleaned and cleaned and cleaned—tackling every room in Cheryl's house, then looking for more. Although I was exhausted, I didn't even stop to sleep because sleeping meant that for one minute before closing my eyes, I would feel my feelings—and I was sure that one minute would kill me.

Mom walked into the kitchen while I was cleaning it—again. "Why are you still up?" she asked. "Tomorrow's a long day, and you should be in bed sleeping."

"I'm just cleaning, Mom." I answered. "I'm not really tired."

I didn't want to alarm her by telling her how hard a simple thing like breathing had become, and how I felt like I was suffocating.

She came and stood next to me by the sink, pulled my hands out of the dishwater and gently began to dry them. It felt so good to feel her touch and as I looked into her eyes, I recognized a familiar something in them. Pain. My pain... She stared deep into my eyes as though she were searching for an answer to her own pain, then suddenly her gaze became one of understanding and I knew in that moment that she understood me more than I could ever imagine.

"She knows," I thought. "She knows."

The look in her eyes changed from understanding to sorrow, as if they were saying *I'm sorry for you and I'm sorry for me*—both at the same time. Then, from sorrow they changed to strength as she said, "We have to be strong, Vera. Remember, God's will not our own will. I'm very proud of you and feel so blessed to be your mother."

She let go of my hands, wiping the tears from her eyes as she continued, "You really need to get some sleep. Grandma usually has tranquilizers with her in her purse. Let me go ask her if you can have one, it will help you sleep," she said—then left the kitchen, in search of the medication that would guarantee her daughter a place in Heaven.

CHAPTER EIGHTEEN

THE WEDDING-NIGHT ROOM

I do. I do agree to be a slave to your desires. I do. I do agree to let myself disappear into a life that I would never choose for myself—if I were allowed to choose. I do. I do agree to be worthless, voiceless, and to suffer quietly while I pretend that I love you.

My wedding took place at one of the church member's homes with about fifty family members in attendance. It was late getting started because I took more time than I should have on a walk-and-talk with God earlier that morning. I lost track of time as I searched for peace for my soul, finally finding it by agreeing to be subservient:

God, I surrender to being Samuel's helpmate. I surrender my own opinion. I surrender all that I am for the sake of your kingdom, for the sake of your glory and for Amy's sake too. Thank you for giving me Amy's children to love and for letting me be a part of their lives. I will be strong, God. I will overcome myself and do your will. Yes, your will.

Dad poked his head in the back room where I was quickly putting on my white dress and fixing my hair. I was almost ready... Samuel, Stella and the family were all waiting for me, and Dad was upset that I was holding up my own wedding.

"Hurry up, sister," he growled. "We need to get this show on the road. Everybody is getting impatient!"

I quickly slipped my shoes on and grabbed my bouquet. Then, walking beside my father, I held onto his arm as he guided me down the hallway and into the living room where I would be sealed to Samuel as his third wife.

This was the big moment I had dreamed about during Amy's big moment. But I never imagined that it would be to the same man. I kept my eyes on her three children, walking ahead of us. Alice and Elise were my flower girls and Andrew was the ring bearer. Samuel had allowed them to be a part of our wedding, but only after he had calmed Stella down—quelled her anger, soothed her temper, probably making promises that might be hard to keep... She had become very possessive of Amy's children and our long struggle began with her fighting to keep them away from me, although Samuel wanted them to be around me. He, too, had noticed how well they responded to me and it soothed his worries about them not having their mother.

In private we had talked about it and he had expressed his concern about Stella being a little rough around the edges and not being very affectionate with them, adding, "I love how you love them, and if something bad should ever happen to me, I would want the children to be raised by you."

It warmed my heart to know he recognized my love for them even though he didn't recognize me as my own person—separate from Amy. His constant comments and comparisons to her made this very obvious. Comments like, "You remind me so much of Amy." Or, "I loved when she wore her hair the way you're wearing yours today." Or, "These taste like cookies she used to make."

Eventually, I became so accustomed to it that if he happened not to make a comment for a day, I would wonder if I had done something wrong. It felt as if he was trying to coax me to be more like her, never wanting me to just be myself. And when he did, I was thankful for my disconnecting technique.

After taking our seats in the front row, and when the designated speakers had finished saying what they had to say, it was time for the marriage vows. Dad was performing the marriage and he asked me, along with Samuel and Stella, to please stand.

First, he had me place my left hand in Stella's hand and then he asked her, "Do you willfully give this young woman onto your husband as his bride?"

She nodded yes, placed my hand into Samuel's hand, then stepped back and sat down in her seat.

Dad proceeded with the wedding vows and covenants of eternal, celestial marriage and then asked both of us if we accepted them.

"I do," Samuel said.

"I do," I said with quiet confidence, trusting that the divine peace I had finally managed to find earlier would stay with me.

As Samuel placed a ring on my finger and quickly kissed my lips, I knew there was no going back. Glancing at Stella, I suddenly felt sorry for her. Then Samuel reached for her, took her hand, pulled her close, and hugged her for a very long time. Eventually, he took my arm, pulled me toward him and Stella, and hugged us both. As he let us go, I briefly looked into her eyes before reaching past Samuel to wrap my arms around her and hug her tight. I needed her to trust, as I did, that we could live a worthy celestial marriage together. Not because it was the way things were supposed to be, but because I really believed we could.

Family members began lining up to congratulate us and amongst them was Mama Louise. She squeezed me tight when she hugged me, softly sobbing. "She's here, she's here," she whispered between sobs. "I can feel Amy's spirit and I know she's here."

I too thought I felt my sister's spirit and her joy for Samuel and their children, truly believing she was grateful to him but even more grateful to me.

After the wedding I went back to Cheryl's house to change and pack my things. Samuel would be taking me to California for five days where a lot of the church members worked in construction, including him. He had left the wedding early with Stella so he could spend a few hours with her before leaving on this trip with me, and I waited impatiently for what seemed like an eternity for him to come and pick me up. My newfound peace quickly slipping away, I was perilously close to having a major anxiety attack. At this point, my fragile state-of-mind had nothing to do with Stella, I just wanted the immediate future to be over with as quickly as possible. What was to come terrified me, but it was inevitable, and I knew it.

Samuel finally arrived and carried my suitcase to the car. He waited in the driver's seat while I said goodbye to my family. I hugged grandma and thanked her for coming, then I hugged Mom. I knew she would be gone when I returned, and I hated saying good-bye to her. I had no idea when I would see her again, which was a very hard thing for me to think about, so I tried not to.

"Are you okay?" she asked, when I finally let her go.

"I'm fine," I answered, knowing that I was supposed to be fine. Now that I belonged to Samuel, and had access to the celestial kingdom through him, I assumed that being fine was no longer a choice—it was a command. A command that I had agreed to obey.

Heading out of town, I was actually happy for Samuel's endless chatter which helped keep my mind preoccupied. Three quarters of an hour later we pulled up to a hotel called Casa de la Luna. And without a care in the world, he let me know that this was the same hotel where he and Stella had spent their first night together.

Like the good wife I was determined to be, I sat in the car and waited while he went into the lobby to pay for the room. He returned a few minutes later holding a key with a room number on it.

As we drove around the back looking for the hotel room he laughed and said, "I think this is the same room I stayed in with her as well."

Seemingly not bothered by it at all, after parking the car and hauling in our suitcases he slipped into the bathroom, leaving me a few minutes to myself.

I sat on the edge of the bed and thought about the only thing I knew that could relate to what was about to happen: The Wade Ordeal... God, I hoped this would be different!

Samuel came out of the bathroom and sat next to me on the bed. I was lost in thought as he started babbling again, saying something about his thirtieth birthday being a couple of weeks away, but I really wasn't paying much attention to his words... You are his now, I silently said to myself. Let him do what he wants to you. He is not Wade, he is your husband and he has the right to do with you as he pleases. Just breathe, Vera. Just breathe.

Samuel stopped talking and leaned into me while kissing my lips. I did not respond, but he didn't seem to notice. Then I quietly surrendered completely as he took me—all the while feeling mortified to be completely naked and exposed.

He stopped for a second and asked me if it hurt.

It did hurt, but I lied and said no. Truthfully, it hurt a lot, but I did not allow myself to tell him, believing that as long as he was getting what he needed from me nothing else mattered. It was over quickly and after a few minutes, while he lay sleeping, I grabbed my clothes and hurried into the bathroom to shower.

I felt horrible, like I was a dirty animal of some sort, and I wondered how in the world I was going to handle letting him do that to me again. I had a strong desire to jump out the bathroom window and run as far away as I could, but I knew that would be silly. He's my husband now, I reminded myself, sure that the more times he did it to me, the faster I'd get used to it. And, of course, it could get me pregnant, which was a happy thought because having a baby of my own would be the most wonderful thing to ever to happen to me. That thought helped me hobble—grimacing in pain—back to the bed, and to my husband who had been my sister's husband, Samuel Saunders: Slayer of innocence, my ticket to Heaven, nephew of our prophet.

Five days felt like forever! The sex continued to be the same as the first time. It was about him fulfilling his desires and needs, and me disconnecting and allowing my body to be used. I felt miserable and in so much pain. My bottom hurt, which made walking as well as sitting almost impossible. Relief was finally mine though, three days later, when my period came. This meant I was unclean and that he could not touch me until it was over. I felt incredibly grateful. But later, after telling him that my period had come, he said, "Speaking of bleeding, are you sure you didn't pass out during that ordeal with Wade?"

"No, I didn't," I answered, upset that he was questioning me about it. "Why are you asking me that?"

"Because you didn't bleed as much as Amy did the first time," he answered.

I felt embarrassed by his comment and didn't feel like explaining that I had been laying on the top sheet where most of the blood ended up. The bloodstains he had noticed, on the bottom sheet, were only a small portion of the bleeding. I had tucked the top sheet with most of the bloodstains on it *under* the mattress so he wouldn't see it. I felt so ashamed for having dirtied the sheets, which is exactly how I felt about my own body. Dirty.

The only good thing about it, I decided, was finally knowing what having sex was. And I knew, without a doubt, that Wade did not rob me of my virginity. Samuel did.

CHAPTER NINETEEN

DIRTY LITTLE SECRETS

One of the greatest truths I have ever discovered is that there are all kinds of people in this world; and there are all kinds of people in this country; and all kinds of people in every city and town; and in those towns, there are all kinds of churches filled with all kinds of people—some claiming to be the holy servants of God. But who they really are, no one really knows.

Samuel had a sister who lived in California, and later that day we stopped by her place to visit. After being there for a few minutes, he asked her if he could borrow her phone to call Stella. He stepped out of the room while he talked to her and returned about twenty minutes later, saying that she had gotten a ride here from Chihuahua. Additionally, he would be leaving me at his sister's house for the night while he spent the night with her.

Actually, I was fine with spending the night on the floor at his sister's house—happy that because of my period he would be leaving me alone and going elsewhere to get his needs met. However, when he asked his sister if it was okay to leave me there for the night and told her where he was going, she tore him up one side and down the other—furious that he would even consider doing such a thing.

"You're leaving your new bride to spend the night on the floor by herself while you run off to spend the night with Stella? That is ridiculous!" she scolded. "You would *never* have considered doing that to Stella; and Amy would have never considered doing what Stella has done by following you here. It is disrespectful to Vera. You need to have the decency to wait until you take her back home before spending a night with Stella!"

Okay, well—peace interrupted. I wish she wouldn't have said anything to Samuel because it made him change his mind, and we both slept on the floor at his sister's house that night.

The drive back home to Mexico was emotionally draining. I learned more personal and negative things about members of our church in one day with Samuel than what I had learned about all of them during my entire life. Up until this point, I had looked at them as God-loving, innocent people who were living God's word. But as Samuel went on with story after story about each of them, my heart sank—traumatized by an ugly truth. Certain members that I had admired and respected were doing things that I never would have suspected or believed about them. Child molestations, sex addiction, men having sex with more than one wife at a time, men with authority stealing machinery and equipment in the name of God, and all sorts of ungodly acts done in the name of religion.

I was appalled! His stories made me realize that the sexual violations I had experienced were quite common. At the time, all I wanted was to be understood—but now I knew how ridiculous that was. Had anyone known about it, they probably would have told me that I was making a big deal out of nothing.

I recalled how Samuel had responded when I shared the Wade ordeal with him. Whether I was a virgin or not was all he had inquired about. There was no concern about my state of mind or my well-being. Compassion was nonexistent—and now I understood why. In the world I lived in, it really was no big deal. Women belong to men. How dare I desire compassion!

I didn't like this new reality. It felt like I was losing my innocence all over again, only this was a different type of innocence—it wasn't so private, and yet it was. My trust in the people I believed and believed in was shattered, and I suddenly felt surrounded by a dark and dirty world, a world where the truth is a lie—a lie wearing a smile; a sinner pretending to be a saint... And these were the people who had the keys to Heaven?

It was all so overwhelming, and I wondered if I would ever feel a ray of sunshine again. But who was I to turn to? Who would be able to help me find the sun? Only God, I told myself, then made a promise to show him where my heart was and do my best to light up the darkness that surrounded me.

We arrived back in Chihuahua late in the afternoon and the first stop we made was at Stella's mother's home. She was taking care of the children while Stella was in California, but now that we were back in town Samuel wanted his children to stay with us—and I couldn't wait to see them!

After parking the car in the front of the house, Samuel walked up to the door and knocked a few times, but no one was home. He returned to the car and drove to the house Stella had moved out of after Amy died and was now to be mine. Before we could get out of the car, the three children came running toward us—full of giggles and hugs. They were so excited to see me, chattering up a storm as they helped me unload the car while Samuel went into the neighboring house (where Stella now lived)—returning a few minutes later, shaking his head with a look of disbelief on his face.

"Stella's mom had the audacity to tell me that I can't have my children stay with you," he fumed. "Stella left her with strict orders not to let me take them because she doesn't want them with you. She's full of baloney! No one is going to tell me what I can and cannot do with my children," he continued, still shaking his head. "They are staying with you, and that's all there is to it. I'll deal with Stella in California when I go back to get her next week."

I couldn't help but notice the look on the children's faces. It clearly was upsetting to them to see their dad so angry. It made me feel slightly uncomfortable—as though I had somehow caused a problem. But Alice seemed to feel my discomfort and, as if she were intentionally trying to make me feel better, she smiled at me and grabbed my hand. Intertwining her chubby little fingers with mine, she pulled me toward the walkway that led to my new home.

Andrew followed us, and when I looked back and smiled at him his face lit up—then, grabbing hold of my other hand, we walked around to the back door of *my* house.

Alice and Andrew were excited about showing me the small, two-bedroom house. It had a living room, a bathroom between the bedrooms, a small kitchen with a pantry, and a dining area. Samuels's mother had lived there for a while and when she moved out, she left a few pieces of furniture behind—including some overstuffed striped couches. I sat down on one of them and both children came up and sat on my lap.

Alice, playing with my hair, said, "Dad said we can call you Mama Vera."

My heart almost jumped out of my chest when she said those unexpected words and a few seconds later Andrew concurred by saying, "Yeah, Dad said we can, Mama Vera!"

I hugged them both feeling honored by the title they had just given me. It symbolized love and respect like the love and respect I had always felt for Mama Vee.

They both giggled and laughed as I began tickling them and it wasn't long before they had wrestled me to the floor trying to tickle me back. We were all laughing so hard that tears were running from our eyes—although my tears were not from being tickled but from my feelings of joy, knowing that I would get to be somewhat of a mom to my sister's children. It meant the world to me and even though they would live with Stella, I would get to be their Mama Vera—the one who would make sure their mother's love would never be forgotten.

After giving my new home a thorough cleaning and filling the cupboards with food, it was ready for us to spend our first night there. It felt a little bizarre knowing that this would be my permanent home from now on—and even more bizarre that I now belonged to Samuel and would be making a life with him here in Chihuahua in this house.

The children spent the night in the second bedroom, across the hall from Samuel and me. When they awoke in the morning, they came into our room and jumped in bed with us. I snuggled with the two girls while Samuel got up and took Andrew outside with him to milk the goats—returning a half-hour later with a two-gallon pail full of fresh milk.

The girls set the table, then all the kids sat down with their dad— ready to enjoy their breakfast together. Flipping the last pancake, I looked up, watching from the kitchen as the stack of pancakes on the table—along with butter and syrup—were passed around... This is Amy's little family, I thought. If only she were standing here instead of me, how different my life would be. If she had not died, I would not be here, and I would certainly not be Samuel's wife. I would not feel this need to protect her children or the obligation to allow myself to be used for Samuel's benefit... The saddest part was my belief that if Amy had not died, he would have never considered marrying me—no matter how many dreams God may have sent to Mom.

As I continued watching Amy's family enjoy their breakfast, I couldn't help but feel a deep sense of sadness. A sadness that haunted me because I knew that Samuel would never get to know me, much less love me. He could *say* he loved me all he wanted, but I knew he didn't and never would because I would never be able to make him happy. I was just a girl whose heart and mind were constantly battling with each other, knowing that if I couldn't make *him* happy, it meant that I couldn't make Dad or God happy either. They were all mixed together as one; and Dad's and God's acceptance were necessary for me to make it to Heaven—and now Samuel's acceptance had been thrown into the mix. So, happy or not, I'll need to be what he wants me to be, I thought. More like Amy. And if I can keep a smile on my face and go at this with a good attitude, no one will ever know the truth of my sadness. Not even God. And I will make it into his kingdom.

CHAPTER TWENTY

THE DUTIFUL WIFE

This world I live in, this world of celestial marriage, this world of sharing a husband, of taking turns—of spreading my legs like a dutiful wife and making the most of "my night"—is the only world I know. And I accept it—because for a woman, it is the only path to Heaven; although, no one has told me yet that the Holy Place I'm trying to get to, is filled with men I despise.

I settled into my role as a dutiful wife rather quickly. My days consisted of more cooking, cleaning and washing, only now, taking care of Samuel's needs had been added to the list.

Samuel believed in being fair and made sure he spent equal time with his two wives. He took turns alternating nights between us and on the nights when it wasn't my turn with him, or "my night" as we called it, one or more of Amy's children would spend the night at my house.

Samuel also spent a lot of time working in California. He was saving whatever money he made and investing it in farms and cattle ranches in Chihuahua. He also equally divided his time with us there, taking one of us each time he went so that we could cook and clean for him while he worked.

Amy's children got to stay with me for four or five weeks at a time when it was Stella's turn to go, and occasionally he would even bring them to the States with us when it was my turn. I loved those times, even though Stella's resistance caused plenty of problems. I still hadn't won her over yet and was beginning to feel like an offender. The more I wanted to do the right thing (hoping our relationship would grow) the harder she pushed against me. Samuel had promised that she would eventually get over her initial jealousy and accept me. And I had believed it, especially since we both were born into polygamy and she had chosen to be a second wife herself.

I often thought about how much I wanted to be her friend, but I just didn't know how to make it happen. Months had gone by and she still wanted nothing to do with me. It concerned me a lot because I believed that if we couldn't get along like good sister wives, my chances of making it into the celestial kingdom were drastically diminished. A few of the prophet's wives didn't get along with each other and for that he never bestowed upon them certain celestial blessings—which was frightening—and I certainly didn't want it happening to me. I had already given up so much, and to fall down right before crossing the finish line terrified me.

On one occasion, Stella invited me to her house to play cards along with some of her friends. I happily agreed—believing our friendship might finally start to grow. But that night, when Samuel stayed with her and sent Alice to my house to spend the night with me, I realized just how naïve I was...

"Mama Vera," she said, "do you know what Mama Stella and her friends were doing while you guys were playing cards today?"

"No," I answered. "What were they doing?"

Seemingly embarrassed, she poked her middle finger up. "They were doing this to you every time you weren't looking," she said. Then, lowering her hand, she looked down as though she was ashamed, adding, "It made me feel sad for you, Mama Vera. I don't like it when people point the bad finger. It's not nice."

Not knowing what to say to her, I decided to change the subject and asked if she wanted me to make her a peach and goat milk shake—which I knew she couldn't resist. And, after climbing up onto the barstool, she sat swinging her feet back and forth while waiting for her shake. Handing it to her, along with a peanut butter and honey sandwich, I watched as she thoroughly enjoyed every sip and every bite—occasionally stopping to lick her sticky fingers.

As I watched her, I was overwhelmed with feelings of love and protectiveness... Bless her heart, I thought. She knows exactly what's going on with Stella and me, and she's stuck in the middle. Actually, all three of the children are stuck in the middle. They are questioned to death about every move I make while they're with me. Then I'm ridiculed in front of them about whatever she judges worthy of ridicule—whether it's that I put too many chocolate chips in my cookie dough, spend too much time with my sisters, buy something she doesn't think I should have, or leave the garden hose running too long when I'm watering the grass... It always seems to be something—and happy as I am that they trust me enough to tell me what Stella says, I don't like that they always end up in the middle of it.

Silently sighing, I decided I needed to try harder, thinking there must be something I could do—or not do—that would make it better. I'll learn to rise above it, I promised myself, and in the meantime, I'll keep my focus on Amy's children and on the child now growing in my belly.

Trying not to, but still thinking about her, it occurred to me that maybe my pregnancy was the reason Stella's behavior had gotten so much worse. It didn't make sense because she was pregnant too—and much further along than I was. But perhaps she felt threatened by the newer, younger wife—who just happened to be me.

Cleaning my way through the rest of the day, eventually I let it go. At the time, I was just too young, too queasy, and too busy dealing with Samuel's non-stop advances to figure it out... As the days flew by, I completely erased it from my mind and, somehow, through it all, I managed to fulfill my role as an always-available-for-your-pleasure wife and an always-trying-harder-to-please-you sister wife.

Late one evening, when it wasn't my night to be with Samuel, I had a few friends over for dinner—something I loved to do whenever I had a little piece of freedom. My friends teased me a lot about how much I talked about my pregnancy and unborn baby, but I didn't care. I was too excited to care about anything else. Having a baby would change my life and I could hardly wait for seven more months to go by!

After dinner, we were having fun playing a card game we all loved. But during the game—which required grabbing a spoon from the table when your face cards matched up—as I stood up and reached for a spoon, I accidentally knocked my chair over. Because we were all laughing so hard, I didn't realize it had fallen over and when I went to sit down again, I landed on the floor. The impact on my tailbone almost knocked the wind out of me leaving me breathless for a few seconds, along with a sharp shooting pain in my abdomen.

When the pain finally subsided, I got up, but as I walked to my bedroom and got in bed, I knew something was wrong. The sharp pain had become a steady dull ache just above my pelvis and I wondered if I had hurt my baby—praying to God, as I laid there crying, that the pain would go away. I couldn't interrupt Stella's night by asking Samuel for help, so I stayed in bed—laying as still as I could—and waited for morning to come.

The next morning the pain had subsided a little, and I thought that perhaps everything was going to be all right—until I went into the bathroom... Blood. Lots of blood, which I knew was a very bad sign when you're pregnant. I began to cry again, praying that I wouldn't lose my baby—the mere thought of it, unbearable.

Later, when Samuel stopped by for his normal morning check-in, he agreed that I should see the local midwife. I did, and she instructed me to go home and rest. I was indeed having a miscarriage, she informed me, and there was nothing that could be done.

Losing my baby—a baby I wanted with all my heart—was a devastating experience. I laid on the couch sobbing, wondering why God would take my baby away from me. The emotional pain was far greater than the physical pain, and I just couldn't understand why I would be given such a wonderful gift, only to have it ripped away. Then, suddenly, I told myself to stop crying—that it wasn't going to change anything, and that God had more important things to do than worry about me getting what I wanted.

Drying my tears, I pictured God, who I still could not separate from my own dad, preaching sermons to all his sons about his kingdom and the important role they all played in it. There was not one woman amongst the hundreds of men I envisioned God talking to; and, in that moment I did not think to question it. I simply believed that this was how God operated. He was too busy for a silly girl like me because he was busy with those of his children that really mattered. His sons.

Blessed is he who has his quiver full of sons, is a Bible quote that I'd heard often. Sons help build a man's posterity not only here on Earth but in Heaven as well, unlike daughters who are given away by their fathers only to help in the building up of some other man's posterity. No wonder the competition amongst the sister wives to bear the most sons was fierce—unspoken, but fierce nonetheless. The women believed that the more sons they gave birth to, the more of their husband's favor and love they would receive. And this, of course, was important in securing a position with their husbands.

I prayed that when Stella delivered, she would give birth to a boy—believing that if she had Samuel's next son, she would feel more secure with him and would lighten up on me. Maybe then things would get better between us. My world would change and I wouldn't feel so alone in this marriage, and maybe I could open up to her about how I really felt about Amy's kids. If I did, she might understand that I wasn't trying to take anything away from her. After all, I never wanted to take my sister's children from her, and I didn't want to take Samuel from her either. I just wanted to live celestial marriage and to love Amy's children in the process, as I promised I would. I longed for us to move forward in a positive direction—one of connection and respect—and I wanted to tell her that I didn't want to rob her of anything, I just wanted to be her friend... Someday, I thought. But that someday was nowhere near.

Stella soon gave birth to a beautiful little girl. And, although Samuel loved his daughters, he made it clear he wanted a boy... It had been three months since my miscarriage. My period was late, and I was hopeful that I was pregnant again—but I didn't let myself get too excited until enough time had passed for me to know for sure.

According to my pregnancy book my baby was due on December tenth, which made me incredibly happy because Andrew's birthday was December first, and the thought of giving him a brother or sister so close to his birthday was exciting... I had a strong feeling that I was having a boy, and after three missed periods I stopped in to see the midwife and get a checkup—confirming that I was pregnant again.

My baby was all I thought about, even though dark things were happening all around me... More polygamist marriages, psychological abuse of women, radical perspectives in our church meetings, fighting amongst the members as to who held the priesthood, alcoholism, sexual perversion, more abuse, more marriages—and, more apparent than anything else, the sadness I noticed on most of the women's faces. I understood none of it, but I didn't question it much either. I just accepted it all as God's way.

Thoughts of being a mother consumed me and December came before I knew it. My labor pains began late on the eve of the seventh. I had arranged for Mama Vee to be with me during the birth of my baby and was so glad I did. As the pains got stronger, I could feel her love for me getting stronger too.

As I walked around the house between contractions, I felt uncomfortable with Samuel there watching me. He was nervous, and I could sense it. His impatience was getting the best of him and he kept asking the midwife to check me to see how far I had advanced—which was painful and embarrassing. But, being the good wife, I simply breathed through it all—trying not to let his anxiousness distract me.

When it was finally time to push, I realized that I had somehow missed the part in the birth book where it explained how much it was going to hurt. I was under the impression that the only pain I would feel would be from the contractions, but as the baby began to crown, I quickly realized I had missed something. Crying out in pain, I immediately felt guilty for expressing my agony, as though it was a sign of being weak. But one more push and my beautiful baby boy was born before dawn on December eighth. As the midwife placed him in my arms, I experienced the most complete and amazing feeling of love which, up until that moment, I had never known was possible.

I knew my life with Stella was about to get harder because I had just given Samuel a son, but I didn't care. All that mattered now was my baby. He was finally here, and he was healthy. Mama Vee put her arm around my shoulders and kissed my forehead as the midwife took the baby from me to weigh and measure him. I looked around the room—my eyes searching for Samuel—but he was nowhere to be seen. Not surprisingly, he had gone to deliver the news to Stella.

With Samuel out of the room, I allowed myself to express my feelings and for a few minutes I just laid there weeping with joy. All

I could think about was how wonderful it was that my baby was finally here—and I couldn't wait to hold him again.

Matthew Thomas would be his name. Together, Amy and Samuel had picked out this name in case they had another boy—and it was decided by Samuel to give this name to his next born son regardless of who gave birth to him. Although I had no say in the matter, the fact that my sister had a say in it made me feel better. Knowing *she* had something to do with the naming of my son gave me a sense of pride and made me feel as if we were on the same team.

Even though my sister wife couldn't stand me, and Samuel didn't know me, I knew Amy loved me—and as time went on, whenever Stella's jealous escapades made my life miserable, I held onto the belief that Amy was close by and understood me. I truly believed she knew how I was feeling and that she was sending me love and support from Heaven—and it was this unwavering belief that helped me through the worst of times with Stella.

On one occasion, when Samuel went to California for a family event—and it was my turn to accompany him—Stella decided to meet up with him before my turn was officially over... Definitely a man of economy—especially when he was traveling—Samuel never seemed to realize that he was the creator of many of the problems that existed between his wives. And, although it was customary in celestial marriage for each wife to have their own private space (either their own house or their own room if they shared a house which would make their *own bed* the sacred place they shared with only him), Samuel didn't seem to mind staying in the same room and sleeping in the same bed with each of us on our turns with him. That one wife was going out the back door while another was coming through the front door, didn't bother him a bit! But I eventually got used to it—not because I wanted to, but because I had to—even though it caused a mountain of problems, especially on this particular trip.

I was busy packing my things and getting ready to leave when Stella arrived—much earlier than she was supposed to—and I was surprised when I found her sitting in the front room. She couldn't move her things into the bedroom until I was gone and seemed annoyed that I hadn't left yet. Not wanting to cause any problems, I said hello to her as I walked through the front room into the laundry room to retrieve my final load of clothes from the dryer. Looking at me as though she wanted to kill me, I instantly felt uncomfortable, although I tried not to show it. Instead, I said a few words about the house we were staying in as I passed through the room—that the owner was nice enough to rent a clean room to Samuel even though the rest of the house was messy.

Stella said something to me, but I couldn't make out what she had said, and when I walked back through the front room, she was no longer there. Instead, she was outside talking to Samuel and a couple of his sisters who were visiting. Wanting to get out of there as quickly as I could, I continued packing my things. Almost done and ready to go, Samuel suddenly burst into the room yelling at me.

"Why were you so fucking stupid? You should have never said anything to Stella! Now you look like a damn fool to my sisters and it embarrasses the hell out of me!"

I immediately stopped what I was doing and stared at him. What he was saying didn't make sense and confused me. "What in the world are you talking about?" I asked.

"Stella said you told her off."

"Told her off?" I repeated, confounded by the accusation. "I didn't say anything other than how messy the house was."

"Well, she says you told her off!"

"And you believe her? You really believe her?"

"I don't know what to believe." he answered. "It's your word against hers."

Stunned, I felt a wave of anger wash over me. I was tired of always having to defend myself—and I'd had enough of Stella's wild rants. "Believe whatever you want to believe," I muttered, going back to my packing.

All I wanted to do was get away from both of them. Stella obviously didn't care about celestial marriage and never would—and I was beginning to wonder why I cared. I asked myself again and again why it mattered to me. It was nothing but problems and more problems, pain and more pain—and yet to see it through was the only way for me to get to Heaven, so I needed to figure out how to make it work.

Closing my suitcase, I almost convinced myself that I was to blame for the incident by having spoken to her at all. But then her lying came to mind again—and this certainly wasn't the first time she had lied, nor would it be the last—and I felt myself plummeting into that angry place I always tried so hard to stay away from. There was no reason for her to lie to Samuel about me and I was tired of defending myself. The whole thing was vicious nonsense and for the first time I could not let go of it—which led to a year of us not speaking to each other at all.

It was a difficult year, but I learned a lot about the reality of Stella, and eventually my desire to be her friend faded into a more realistic desire to just keep the peace. But, of course, Samuel continued to make excuses for her, saying that she had a harder time with celestial marriage because she didn't care about the gospel like I did. And that makes it okay, I wondered... Okay to lie? Okay to be cruel? Okay to manipulate every situation to her own advantage? It was a bitter pill to swallow, but I kept swallowing it—to keep the peace, I just closed my eyes and swallowed until the day Samuel came home and demanded that I fix my relationship with her.

"Vera," he announced—his face flushed with humiliation, "you need to go and make peace with Stella. I was just over visiting with some of the guys and they asked me if it was true that my wives hadn't spoken to each other for over a year. I admitted it was true, and Carl really laid into me. He wanted to know what in the hell kind of man I was that I couldn't make my wives talk to each other. It really embarrassed me when they laughed and teased me about not being man enough to lead my family and to make my wives do what I say. So please go talk to her, Vera. Just do it."

I knew why he had asked me to do it and not Stella. He knew I cared. And she didn't. So the following morning I buried my pride beneath a pile of dirty clothes and vowed to do the right thing by going to visit her.

She answered the door and as soon as she saw me, she laughed and said, "He got you to do it, huh?"

As if it were a joke, she just stood there laughing, but I honestly didn't care if she thought it was funny. All I wanted to do was please Samuel by doing what he had asked me to do—and what he wanted was for me to break the ice, kiss up to her, and save him from further embarrassment. Which I did. And now that I had, he could go back to his male friends and brag about how he rules his family, and his wives do whatever he tells them to do. Well, one of them does anyway!

Sadly, I was nowhere close to living celestial marriage the way I had believed I would. This holy arrangement was a sham—more like two women pushing against each other trying to live monogamously with a polygamist man. I didn't like it, but I accepted it. After all, I had no choice but to accept it, because a polygamist wife either accepts it all or she burns in hell.

A few days later, Samuel stopped in to visit me for a few minutes before heading over to Stella's for the night. He seemed down—like something was bothering him. Not really knowing how to ask him what was wrong, I said nothing. And, while he laid back on the couch staring mindlessly at the ceiling, I gave my attention to the television. Then—out of nowhere—he suddenly cried out, "I hope I die before you or Stella so I can have some alone time in Heaven with Amy!"

I was caught off guard by his anguished remark but sensed he was longing for her. "I hope you get some time alone with her too," I said sympathetically—truly hoping they would have a long time together before I arrived.

His face was wrought with sadness as he looked over at me and searched for something in my eyes. My heart went out to him, but I knew he would not find in my eyes what he was looking for. Getting up, he came over to my side and kissed my cheek before leaving.

I never let him kiss my lips anymore. Whenever he tried, I turned my head to the side, ensuring that his kisses would land in a place I was more comfortable with. It was actually the only thing I had any control over... Lips or cheek? And I chose cheek every time.

After he left, I no longer paid attention to the TV. My thoughts were all about Heaven and the implications of what he had just said. I was fully aware that celestial marriage was a requirement to enter God's kingdom, but I had never imagined being together in Heaven as a family with Samuel, Amy, and Stella. It was a terrifying thought, and it didn't feel right at all! I had joined Samuel's family to make it to the celestial glory and for the sake of Amy's children, but I had pictured myself in Heaven, free from him once he and my sister were together again. I couldn't imagine being his wife with Amy in the picture! I just couldn't. And the thought of being in an eternal family with Stella scared the hell out of me!

For the first time, what I had done by marrying him hit me with the force of a hurricane! Being in Samuel and Stella's family was hell, and I realized that I had joined hell in order to join God in Heaven where my hell would be eternal! I needed to talk to Dad so he could help me understand... I can handle being married to him right now in order to make it to Heaven, I thought, but I refuse to be his wife in eternity.

The following evening I stopped at Mama Vee's house to visit, with the intention of talking to Dad about this whole eternal marriage to Samuel thing. I knew I had agreed to marry him, but I never intentionally agreed to be his eternal wife.

Dad was sitting at the dining room table eating crackers when I arrived and, after hugging him and Mama Vee, I sat down at the table with them. Not surprisingly, it didn't take long for Dad to start in on his judgments of the evils in the world, starting with me. He looked at the capris I was wearing—stopping a few inches above my knees—then he took a look at my short-sleeved blouse.

"It is because of women dressing the way you're dressed that AIDS exists in the world," he stated with disgust, pointing at me.

I didn't dare say anything back to him and sat in my chair feeling extremely uncomfortable about his radical statement.

"What has gotten into you women these days?" he asked, as if he really wanted to know.

I didn't care to discuss what had or had not *gotten into me,* although I really wanted to know what I had *gotten myself into* (eternally) by marrying Amy's husband. But I couldn't out and out ask him, so I decided to speak in general terms.

"Dad," I began, gingerly brushing right past his question, "is it possible to go to Heaven by living celestial marriage on earth with someone, but not staying married to that person once you get there?"

He looked at me as though my question amused him, then quickly went into an explanation of what he passionately believed about marriage…

"Once you marry someone, you belong to that person in this life, the next life, and throughout all eternity. In God's eyes, there is no such thing as divorce on earth much less in Heaven," he said. "Humans get divorced in this world all the time, but God doesn't allow it. They are only fooling themselves and therefore committing more sin against God by causing each other to commit adultery when remarrying. Your question is a very silly question, sister. There is no divorce in God's eyes and we will all be with our spouses forever. Don't you agree?"

I did not agree, but in fear, I said I did. I had never questioned any of Dad's religious explanations before, but this time I felt deep in my soul that he was wrong. I could feel it; and I knew that being Samuel's wife eternally was an eternal lie! I don't know how I knew it, especially when it went against everything Dad had just explained to me, but I knew.

Even though I was sure he was wrong, my father's explanation had left me feeling unsettled. And when I returned home, I thought about it more which brought forth more questions—questions I had never even thought of asking before. But unfortunately, I had no answers—so I decided to push the whole topic to the back of my mind and focus on Amy's children and my own growing family.

Another missed period let me know I was pregnant again. Stella had given birth to another daughter and an announcement of me being pregnant right now would not be favorable for me, so I made the decision to hide my pregnancy for as long as possible. This, of course, meant that I had to hide it from Samuel too. He never could keep a secret and the longer I was married to him, the more obvious it became. He shared intimate things with me about Stella that I knew she wouldn't want me to know, always following it with, "Don't tell anyone." Or, "She didn't want me to tell you."

It finally dawned on me that he was probably doing the same thing to her regarding me, which he did admit to when I confronted him with it. I couldn't trust him, and I didn't. I knew that anything that went on between us was always going to be Stella's business as well. So I didn't tell him I was pregnant, nor did I tell anyone else—not even the midwife. I wanted to put off the repercussions from Stella for as long as possible—I just couldn't take the chance of her finding out yet. And although I was ecstatic about having another baby, I felt very much alone. My breasts were tender, and my tummy was starting to swell. I was concerned that Samuel might notice when he had his way with me, but he rarely fully undressed me—so my secret was safe for a while.

CHAPTER TWENTY-ONE

THE WEDDING-DEATH DAY

There are no walls between us, only an unlocked door that is both and entrance and an exit. And, sometimes, those coming in collide with those going out.

It is the middle of December and the weather has turned cold. A few snowflakes have fallen and the smell in the air from all the wood-burning heaters is strong. I have new resentments, blossoming questions, old beliefs, and an ancient habit of convincing myself that what I feel doesn't matter because I am not worthy of mattering.

It is Bonita's wedding day and I'm feeling a bit of resentment towards God. She is marrying the man of her dreams. He is the same age she is—and he has the same desire for a monogamous union as she does. In the eyes of a polygamist, it is all wrong. And yet Bonita is radiant with joy and no one seems to notice that it isn't right.

My thoughts haunt me. I don't understand why God is allowing her to marry her childhood sweetheart, because when I wanted to marry mine, I was denied the right to do so. "It doesn't seem fair, God," I said out loud as I sat in front of the mirror curling my hair. "Why did she get to say no to marrying Samuel, but I didn't? Why did I have to give up Gregario to live celestial marriage, yet she doesn't have to live celestial marriage at all? Why God?"

Not wanting to be heard questioning God, I closed my mouth—thinking, instead of speaking... Bonita and I are the same age, raised in the same family, and taught the same principles, and yet I'm living a totally different lifestyle than what she is permitted to live. It just doesn't make sense.

As a tidal wave of unworthiness washed over me, I finished curling my hair and getting dressed. Still struggling with the unfairness of it all, I didn't let it go until Samuel walked through the door—letting me know it was time to go. Knowing it would take us at least forty-five minutes to get there, I hurried out to the car and sat in the front passenger seat. A few minutes later, Stella walked up to the car and scowled at me because I was sitting in the front seat. Then, giving me a dirty look, she opened the door and sat in the back.

Oh boy, I thought, it's going to be a long night... I had always struggled with motion sickness but being pregnant made it ten times worse and I knew if I sat in the back seat I would be in trouble. The last thing I wanted was to ask Samuel to stop the car in case I needed to throw up, which would expose my secret to both of them. So I chose to take my chances and ride in the front, knowing it would cause a problem for Stella—but a small upset now was better than a big blow-up later, which would happen as soon as she found out about my pregnancy. Her jealousy was volatile, and I did not want to deal with it today.

We arrived at the wedding along with about two hundred other guests, then found a table where we could sit and have dinner with our family and friends. Bonita looked beautiful and was glowing from head to toe as she smiled and danced with her new husband, James. The music was loud and a few of the church members were beginning to drink a little too much—including my brother-in-law, Shem. He had two wives, one of which was my half-sister, Diane. She was Mama Louise's next born daughter after Amy, and she had brought her own two daughters with her—Cassandra, who was seven and Megan, who was five months old—along with Shem, whose mother and sister tagged along as well.

I watched Diane from my table as she made a noticeable effort to look happy while her husband danced the night away with an unmarried teenage girl. With a glum look not so well hidden in her eyes, she left her table several times to go nurse her baby in the powder room—but I was sure her frequent disappearances were to try to get ahold of her emotions. She looked very sad... Her husband, Shem, was not an easy man to live with and her sister wife was even worse. She suffered immensely and had tried several times to leave him but every time, after taking counsel from Dad, she would go back. Divorce seemed like an impossible option even though he had physically abused her more than once. As I sat and observed her face, I could see that the light in her eyes had completely vanished. Celestial marriage had taken her sunshine and replaced it with an alcoholic, physically abusive, womanizing husband who somehow was supposed to be her key to the celestial kingdom.

As I continued to connect with her inner-suffering, it reminded me of my own. Although her life was slightly different from mine, the sorrow part was identical. I had noticed this same sadness in the eyes of many polygamist women in our town but assumed it was because, as women, we didn't try hard enough to overcome our weak minds and sad thoughts. But tonight Diane's eyes reflected something hidden deep inside my own soul.

I desperately wanted to shield her from what I knew she was feeling, but how does one shield another's sadness? Thinking about how much I wanted to help her, a dark feeling washed over me, and a sense of hopelessness settled in as I accepted the fact that there was nothing I could do. We are in the same sinking boat, I thought, but at least I know how to swim. And maybe if I keep paddling as hard as I can before the boat goes down, and if I stay strong in spite of my own circumstances, I can at least help her to feel understood.

Hanging onto the small bit of hope that I could do something to ease her suffering, I followed her into the bathroom, wanting to have a minute alone with her. She was busy changing Megan's diaper and didn't notice me until she looked up and caught me watching her in the mirror. Smiling as she finished changing her baby, she handed her to me before going into one of the stalls. I was glad to help and bounced her baby in my arms until Diane came back for her. The bathroom was crowded with women waiting for their turn to use the stalls, and it didn't feel like the right time to tell her what I had wanted to tell her, so we talked about the wedding instead as we both made our way back into the reception area.

A few hours later, Samuel decided it was time for us to go home. More than happy to be leaving because I was worried about my own sweet baby—at home with a babysitter. I hugged Bonita goodbye and went out to the car. Samuel was already sitting in the driver's seat and, again, I got in beside him. Next, came Queen Stella. Then all hell broke loose.

Refusing to sit in the back, she exploded with anger. "I'm not going home if she doesn't sit in the back!" she yelled.

Out of the car and trying to calm her down, Samuel walked around to my side of the car saying, "Vera, just ride in the back. Please! It is her night, and you already had a turn riding in the front with me. She's threatening to find another ride home if you don't sit in the back. You know she makes a big deal about this kind of stuff and you should know better by now."

He was right. I did know better, but I was hoping for a miracle—praying she would overlook it just this once. I didn't care about sitting next to Samuel like she did. I only cared about not throwing up and revealing my secret. Stella could have him, tonight and every night, for all I cared. But I wasn't about to explain anything to either one of them, so I just did as I was told while Stella raged on; reprimanding me as if I was a two-year-old, telling me how selfish and inconsiderate I was and that I needed to learn some respect.

There were so many things I wanted to say to her. She had made living celestial marriage more difficult than I ever thought it would be and I was so tired of walking on eggshells. Her constant judgments were beginning to break me, and I wished she'd just leave me alone. But she went on and on and on, until I finally blurted out, "You're such a baby!"

Surprised by my own words, I sat back in silence. I knew I shouldn't have said it, and I felt guilty for lashing out at her, but at least it got her to stop her incessant rant. But Samuel wasn't quite so quiet, following my outburst with, "You're both damn babies!"

Indeed we are, I thought... How we were living was not the celestial marriage I had imagined—and it certainly wasn't how my parents lived the principle. I had always pictured a sister wife as a friend, and I had pictured a husband who was fair and who understood the value of integrity. The hatred, humiliation and jealousy from Stella, along with the pressure from Samuel to cater to her insecurities, was getting harder and harder to handle. The emptiness within me was growing day by day, and the longer I was married to him the more alone I felt.

It was a long drive home and when we finally pulled into Stella's driveway, I felt relieved as she and Samuel got out of the car and went into the house together. Slipping into the driver's seat—because I had to drive to the babysitter's house to pick up my son, Matthew—I felt the stark reality of loneliness pierce my heart. It was very late at night—dark and cold—and relieved as I was to be rid of the two people who made my life miserable, driving to the babysitter's house alone suddenly seemed like an impossible task. I was exhausted—completely drained of any dignity I might have ever possessed—and it felt as if my soul was disappearing.

In that moment, I longed for a *real* husband. One who did not go into his "other wife's house" and leave me sitting alone, shivering in the black night. A husband who wanted to share a life with me—one who treated me like I meant something, cared about my thoughts and feelings, and who truly loved me... I wondered if there even was such a thing; and as I wondered, I let my longing go.

After picking Matthew up, I somehow managed to drive home, change his diaper, and crawl into bed—stripped of all hope of a different life, too tired to even think about it and resigning myself to a marriage that did nothing but make me feel unloved and unwanted.

I had just closed my eyes when I heard someone relentlessly banging on my front door. Filled with fear, I jumped out of bed, ran into the kitchen, and stood with my back against the wall next to the door.

My heart pounded as I gathered up enough courage to yell, "Who is it?"

The banging continued—rattling my bones—so I shouted louder, "What do you want?"

"Vera, its Mama Nadine. Please open the door," she pleaded.

Wondering what in the world was going on I quickly opened the door—stunned by the sight of Mama Nadine standing in her bathrobe sobbing, "Diane is dead, Vera, she's dead!"

Shocked and trying to make sense of what she was saying, I asked, "What do you mean Diane is dead?"

"She's dead, Vera, and so is Megan. Shem was driving his family home from the wedding—but he was drunk and lost control of his truck. It caused a terrible accident. Little Cassandra and Shem are doing okay, but his mother is in critical condition. And his sister, along with Diane and Megan, didn't make it."

Her sobbing continued as she added, "Ask Samuel if he can help us. Bonita is at home, laying on my couch in total shock—and she can't stop crying. I don't know what to do!"

"Samuel isn't with me tonight," I said, still stunned. "He's with Stella."

With all my heart I wanted to help, but I didn't dare go to Stella's house to tell Samuel that my sister had died. I needed to respect her night. So, stepping outside with her, I encouraged Mama Nadine to go herself—hoping she would understand why I couldn't.

Mama Nadine glanced back at her own house, then ran toward Stella's—still sobbing.

Going back inside and locking the door behind me, I stood in the kitchen trembling as the shock of Diane's death hit me like a ton of bricks. Reeling with grief, my legs gave out beneath me and I fell to the floor... Diane? Dead? No! Not another sister!

I couldn't do anything but lay on the floor and cry—sorrow rushing through my heart as an endless stream of thoughts ran through my mind... Diane was the mother of four children. Three, now that Megan was gone. Who would take care of them now? Shem is obviously not capable of something like that, which eliminates the possibility of them living with him and his first wife.

I found myself wanting to take care of them the same way I had wanted to take care of and love Amy's children... Oh my word, I thought, suddenly realizing that I was living the same scenario over again—only this time it was with a different sister.

Seeping out of my soul, the deepest loneliness I had ever felt rampaged through me. I wanted somebody to wrap their arms around me and hold me tight. I didn't want to be strong right now. I felt weak, and I needed for that to be okay... "God, please," I cried out, "can somebody hold me? Just hold me?"

It might appear to the members of our religious community that I had a husband who would comfort me in a time like this, but only I knew I didn't really have a true husband. I longed to be loved, cared for, and nurtured in the same way I loved, cared for and nurtured others. But my longing was unacceptable—nothing but a hollow wish—so I picked myself up off the floor and, on wobbly legs, walked back to my bedroom.

Crawling into bed next to my son, I picked him up and laid him on my chest. Putting one hand on my tummy as I held him with the other, I drew comfort from the only source I knew would always be there for me—my precious babies: One, snuggled up against me. The other, not yet born. Both, the only part of my life that made any sense. Each, allowing me to experience what real love feels like.

Gently patting Matthew's back, I told myself that even though I had lost another sister and was stuck in a messed up celestial marriage, I still had a lot to be grateful for. And I *was* grateful. My two babies, I thought, and Amy's three children are all I have and all that really matters—they are the only part of my life that feels real and right and safe to me.

Thankful for the beautiful child curled up in my arms, I listened to the commotion going on outside. Vehicles starting and stopping, car doors opening and closing, and voices echoing through the night as the news spread about the accident and the deaths. It all felt so close, and yet so far away as I laid there thinking about Diane—her life, her children, her suffering, her death and the life hereafter. Then thoughts about Bonita and the terrible pain she must be feeling invaded my mind... Losing a sister on her wedding day. She must be falling apart right now—torn between joy and sorrow; between a happy life with the man she loves and a sad life without the sister she loves. How does one decide which feeling to take with them as they continue living? How does one experience the having and the not having at the same time?

I recalled having envied her earlier in the day and what I thought was her struggle-free life. So happy just a few hours ago, and now suffering terribly. Sighing, I told myself that everybody has their struggles in life and perhaps, while handling my own, I should spend a little more time being thankful for everything in my life— whether it makes me smile or simply makes me strong.

The funeral was huge. There were hundreds of family members and friends gathered together, leaning on each other trying to cope with the tragedy. And it was, indeed, a tragedy. God had taken four of his daughter's home, including Shem's mother who had died shortly after arriving at the hospital... The man had lost his mother, his sister, his wife and a daughter all in one night, and the guilt he suffered afterward almost killed him.

Watching him go through the agony of blaming himself was heart wrenching, but the change that came over his heart was inspiring... He reconfigured his whole perspective on life, love, religion and women in general—and turned his life around completely. His spirit and attitude became one of humbleness and compassion; and I often wished that all the men in our community could have a life altering experience such as he had. One that would help change their disrespect and disregard for women and their feelings into something a little gentler—a little kinder—a little less selfish and a lot more caring... Diane was the catalyst of that change for Shem and although she sacrificed her own life to do it, I couldn't help but admire and feel proud of her.

Mama Louise lived across the street from Shem's second wife, Rachel, who wanted nothing to do with Diane's children. So, Shem agreed to let Mama Louise raise them, knowing that by being across the street, he would be able to see them often—and he did. It took some time for them to adjust to a life without their mother, but they eventually got used to living with their grandmother. She was good to them, and I did whatever I could to show them love as well—and I didn't need to marry their father to do it!

CHAPTER TWENTY-TWO

BOBBY

What is not broken, might break.
What is broken, will heal.

It was August 6, 1992. I was busy canning as many jars of peaches as possible. My baby was due to be born in four days and I wanted to get all my canning finished before then. After peeling, pitting and slicing peaches all day, I had managed to put up eighty quart-jars and had another twenty or so to go. And although I had been feeling light contractions for a few hours and felt exhausted, I continued to work hard, trying to get the task done.

By ten o'clock that night I was so tired that I couldn't even imagine pushing a baby out after such an exhausting day, so I sat down on a chair holding the last bowl of peaches to be peeled on my lap. As I did, I could feel a contraction coming on but this one was a lot stronger than the others. Setting the bowl of peaches on the table, I placed my hands on my belly as I breathed through it. The contraction began to ease, and I whispered to my unborn child, "Please wait until tomorrow, sweetheart. Mommy is way too tired tonight."

After it subsided, I returned to peeling peaches and finished filling the last few jars. Matthew was already sleeping and Samuel was at Stella's for the night, so after shutting off the stove and turning out the lights I crawled into bed. And, oddly enough, my baby must have heard my request because the contractions stayed away until the next morning.

I awoke at six o'clock, feeling sharp labor pains. I felt somewhat rested and was ready to face another delivery knowing that I would soon be holding my baby. Mom was still living in Quintana-roo and Mama Vee was out of town, so when the midwife suggested bringing her friend along to help with the delivery, I agreed. I didn't know anything about her, but she seemed like a loving woman.

My labor lasted all day and once again Samuel, impatient as ever, kept asking the midwife to check me every few minutes. The midwife could sense that it was bothering me, so the next time he asked, she winked at me and said, "How about we check you first, Samuel?"

He chuckled as she laughed, and he didn't ask her again throughout the rest of my labor.

At five o'clock in the evening I started to bear down. It seemed like I was having a harder time than I did with Matthew. But I had promised myself that this time I would be stronger and not show any signs of my suffering—so I didn't utter a single word until after the head was out and it was time to birth the shoulders. Suddenly, it felt like the midwife had put her hand up inside me and was gently twisting a shoulder back and forth. This unexpected turn of events scared me, so I stopped pushing and asked her what was happening.

"Everything is fine," she assured me. "Come on, push."

Following her instructions, I pushed until the shoulders finally gave way—and my second beautiful son was born. His little cry was healthy and strong, and as I listened, I began to cry myself. The midwife placed him in my arms and I immediately felt the pure love of another precious child. A little brother for Matthew, I thought, staring at his dark hair and chunky little body. He was so perfect even though his crying seemed to go on much longer than normal—

right along with mine. I was worried about Samuel seeing how weak I really was, but I couldn't seem to control it. And, surprisingly, he didn't leave—he just stood there smiling from ear to ear, obviously excited about having another son.

This time I was allowed a say in naming our son, providing it was a name that could be pronounced in Spanish as well as in English. So I chose Robert Michael with Bobby for a nickname.

The following morning, when I was holding him in my arms trying to nurse him, I noticed that he was allowing one arm to hang instead of bringing it up to his little face like his other arm. But when I picked it up and gently moved it toward his face, he cried—and no matter which way or how gently I moved it, he continued to cry. Sensing that something was wrong, I quickly undressed him and looked at his arm. I couldn't see anything, but as soon as I moved it again, he wailed.

Not about to bother him, I waited for Samuel to drop in for his usual morning visit—anxious to have him bring the midwife back to check on Bobby's arm—which he did. And, after examining him, she concluded that he had somehow hurt his shoulder or arm during birth. I recalled the moment she had put her hand up inside me and had been moving it back and forth, which she must have done to help him straighten out his arm—but because I kept pushing, I must have hurt him somehow. The midwife suggested taking him to a clinic—but it was Sunday and no clinic was open, so I had to wait another day before someone could tell me what was wrong.

Samuel arranged for his sister-in-law to drive me into town the next day. With the excuse of too many things to get done at his farm, he said he couldn't take me—which was definitely not what I wanted to hear. That he believed all duties pertaining to the raising of the children are the wife's responsibility, I understood—but I didn't understand his disregard of me and how I might be feeling. Having a baby wasn't just a walk in the park and dealing with the aftermath of labor while trying to deal with a long drive *and* a baby who cried every time we drove over a bump or pothole, was overwhelming. Needless to say, I found myself longing for a real husband again, noticing that this longing was happening more often.

After arriving at the hospital and having x-rays of Bobby's shoulder and arm taken, the doctor informed me that his upper arm was broken—not cracked but broken all the way through the bone. Immediately followed by the earth-shattering questions, "Did you drop him? How did this happen?"

"No, I didn't drop him!" I exclaimed—quickly telling him what I had felt during his birth.

With that information, the doctor concluded that his arm must have been twisted behind him, and what I had felt was him struggling to rearrange it while in the birth canal. And, as I had suspected, that by pushing without waiting for him to adjust it I had caused it to break.

"We cannot put a cast on it at this young age," he added, "but we'll wrap it across his chest with a band to stop the movement and hold it still so it can heal."

Then, gently touching my shoulder as the tears welled up in my eyes, he said in Spanish, "Don't worry, Señora, your baby is going to be just fine. Babies heal super-fast. Bring him back in a month so we can see how he's doing."

Giving me a comforting smile, he shook my hand before leaving the room. I breathed a sigh of relief at his encouraging words. Even though he was being paid for his services, in that moment of compassion, I felt more support and understanding from a total stranger than I could ever remember feeling from my own eternal husband.

As the days passed, although I continued to feel alone, disconnected and often disrespected, I continued to hold tight to my belief in the eternal salvation of celestial marriage. Being put down and constantly defending myself against Stella wore me out at times, but I was determined to make it to Heaven. I always seemed to find a way of convincing myself that I needed to try harder and overcome my weaknesses—truly believing that if I did, Samuel would care more.

If only I could be more like Amy, I thought, my life would be so much easier. If I had Samuel's support, I wouldn't feel so alone in the raising of my boys.

It was as if I had an unrelenting drive to prove to God, to Dad and to Samuel that I had what it takes to make it to Heaven. Even if it meant suffering my way there, I was going to prove—to every man and male-deity—that I was worthy of Heaven.

CHAPTER TWENTY-THREE

MY FAITH THAT FELT SAFE

*I am who I believe I am—and until I change what
I believe, I cannot change who I am.*

The days are quickly marching onward… Amy's children are getting bigger, along with my two boys. I'm busy doing all the things required of me according to my religion, but I've noticed that with each passing day the numbness I feel is taking up more space inside me. I view it as a blessing because it's the numbness that's helping me survive. I don't know why things are the way they are. I only know that being a mother is the most wonderful thing that has ever happened to me, so I allow myself to feel my feelings only *as a mother*. But as a daughter, a wife and a sister wife, every day I move closer to feeling nothing at all. Thank God.

Becca has married a polygamist man and lives only a few blocks away. We spend a lot of time together. She is a second wife but, unlike me, she is madly in love with her husband. Although celestial marriage has its challenges for her too, she draws strength from her husband and their beautiful connection. His belief system is the same as other cult members, but the love he and Becca have for one another is something very special—like the love Dad and Mama

Vee have for each other. The kind of love everyone around them can feel.

I truly admire Becca's ability to express herself to her husband, and I've recently decided to do the same with Samuel. The mere thought of opening up and sharing my feelings with him scares the living heck out of me, but I'm determined to give it a try. Maybe the emptiness I feel whenever I'm around him is my fault. And maybe I can fix it.

Becca has helped me understand how important it is to share my inner-most feelings with my husband. And as soon as I get a chance, I want to try to do some of the things we've talked about. After role-playing with her a few times, I'm confident that I'll be ready the next time it's my night—and I've decided to start with something small. Becca is sure that if I start with the little things, I'll eventually be able to work my way up to the bigger things. Then the gargantuan things, which terrifies me—but one step at a time seems like good advice.

I don't like that I can never really be myself around Samuel—and imagining a whole lifetime of suppressing my true feelings, as well as my thoughts, dreams and desires is like looking into an eternally gray sky, so I'm determined to try to change things which, of course, is up to me. Samuel certainly doesn't seem to feel responsible for my inner-turmoil, nor does he seem interested in changing anything. So I guess I'm the one who is supposed to take a step toward having a better relationship with him—if you can even call our marriage a relationship. It feels more like a shipwreck. But if there is anything left to salvage, I guess the one without a lifeboat is the one who must dive into the deep, dark sea.

It was my night and it was late. We had just gotten home from a barbecue where many of the church members had gathered together to socialize. After putting the boys to bed, I patiently waited for Samuel to get out of the shower. I really wished I could share all the things I had kept bottled up inside me with him—how I felt used, manipulated, pressured, and emotionally blackmailed by him and Stella; and how he seemed happiest when I simply went along with his needs and desires, unconcerned with how I felt about any of it.

While I sat on the couch in the front room waiting for him, in my mind I envisioned him coaxing me to continue to share my feelings. He was listening, and he actually cared about what I was saying. I even envisioned myself sharing the scariest feeling of all my feelings with him—the one about him using me to replace Amy and what it has done to me. It felt so real and so wonderful to have him care enough to listen, but suddenly—when he walked into the room and sat on the couch across from me—my pretend world turned itself off.

Before I could say a word, he began telling me about one of the member's wives who had attended the barbecue. "She is so outspoken," he complained. "Women like her are disgusting. They always have so much to say, and I can't stand to be around them... Did you hear her tonight?" he added, with a look of disgust on his face.

Emotionally pulling away with a strong sense of shame and guilt because I could see myself in the woman he was talking about, I felt my whole being cringe as my heart recoiled into a safer place.

Whenever I was with Becca or my sisters, I noticed that I could be myself. I was expressive, humorous and sometimes even loud. To hear him state with such adamant disgust that he couldn't stand women like her, made me realize that he wouldn't be able to stand a woman like me either—the real me, not the me who went along with his every whim. In that moment, I decided that trying to open up to him or express myself wasn't possible—and never would be. I couldn't take the chance of him despising me like he despised her.

If my husband rejected me, I firmly believed God would reject me too—and I was well aware of what would happen to my eternal salvation. As I thought about this, I pictured the devil's face with pointy teeth and red horns—laughing, because he had gotten me, rerouted me, and pulled me into an eternal life as the devil's wife, forever facing the fires of an eternal hell!

No, I thought, almost out loud—deciding to keep my feelings buried. Just keep doing what you've been doing, I told myself. It has worked so far, and it is obviously not meant for you to have what Becca and her husband have. So keep yourself together and continue to be strong—sharing your feelings is *not* the answer, overcoming them is. And so I pressed on.

I have just delivered the good news to Samuel that I'm almost five months pregnant and the baby is due on the 19th of July. Once again, he is surprised that I waited so long to tell him about it. And, later that evening, he asked me if I would please not share (with any-body) the fact that he had not known about my pregnancy until now.

"Why?" I asked him, noticing the embarrassed look on his face.

"Because when I told my sister today that you were five months pregnant, she flat out asked me if I had known since the beginning. I told her that of course I did, and she said, 'Wow, I'm impressed. I guess you really can keep a secret.' And I want her thoughts to stay that way," he added, "so please just do it for me."

I nodded my head, letting him know I would do what he asked. I could sense he was happy that I was going to have another child for him, but this time I felt so strongly about it being a girl that I felt that I needed to warn him about it. It felt as if I needed to justify having a daughter by pointing out that I had already had two sons for him.

I wanted a daughter, and I caught myself feeling guilty for believing that I was going to get what I wanted. Noticing, for the first time, that feeling guilty just didn't seem right, I asked myself why I should feel guilty about having a daughter—a daughter that I really wanted. It wasn't just a girl or a boy, it was a human life, and attaching guilt to that was just not something I could easily accept.

After carefully analyzing it, I realized that I had spent most of my life helping and watching others get what they wanted. I didn't know how to receive, without guilt, something that I wanted— which was a precious daughter. It wasn't that I believed her father wouldn't love her, it was that I didn't believe I should be getting what I desired. I was so used to him getting his wants and needs met—at the sacrifice of my own—and I found myself struggling with how to cope with it being the other way around.

I had no control over this at all, and it really bothered me. I couldn't just say, "Here, I'll let it be a boy so you can get what you want." Being meek and mild for the sake of others wasn't going to help in this situation—and boy did I struggle!

I found myself bending over backwards for both Samuel and Stella. I was constantly apologizing—constantly asking for their forgiveness—and, because I did not want to stir up trouble or hurt either of them, I became exceedingly withdrawn. It seemed that no matter what I did or what I said, it was always wrong—so, in an attempt to keep the peace, I simply kept quiet.

Amy's children continued to take turns spending the night with me when Samuel spent the night with Stella, and my love for them grew stronger every day as they grew older. I wasn't withdrawn with them or my own children and, in fact, I noticed how gloriously alive I felt when I spent time with them. I adored them and couldn't imagine my life without them in it.

Occasionally, I found myself daydreaming about Gregario— about what *could* have been. I knew he was married and had started a family of his own, but at times I couldn't help but wonder if he ever thought of me. But each time I did, I quickly reprimanded myself. It was just a dream, not a reality. Samuel was my only reality now, along with Stella. And although my life with them was certainly not the life I would have chosen had I been allowed to choose, it was what it was—however hopeless it seemed.

Normally a positive, cheerful person, as the days passed I felt a weariness creeping into my soul—a weariness I could not shake off. The battle going on inside me was beginning to break my spirit. My quest to be loved and accepted by God, Dad, and Samuel in order to get to Heaven was starting to take its toll on me. When the events of my life would take a swing at me, it was taking me longer than usual to swing back. I was beginning to feel defeated. I wanted to keep trying to fix my weaknesses, but it seemed like the more I sacrificed and the more blame I shouldered, the harder the punches felt.

My self-esteem, self-worth, personal value, dignity and pride had all been stripped from me in the fight and I wondered how much more I'd have to give up before it was enough to enter God's kingdom. What I had been taught, I had never questioned. It was the only thing I knew, and it was my faith in those teachings that felt safe, so I held on. With my whole heart, I held on—truly believing that my faith was who I was.

CHAPTER TWENTY-FOUR

THE GIRL IN THE MIRROR

The mere thought of spending eternity with Samuel, his mother and Stella should have immediately shattered every belief I had ever held dear. But big changes take time, and it took the birth of my daughter—whose value as a human being I would die to protect—for me to realize that it didn't matter if I ended up in Heaven or hell. What would be the difference, I finally asked myself, if I had to spend eternity with them?

It was the middle of July, a hot summer in 1995. Our midwife was easing into retirement by cutting back on the hours she spent delivering babies. Samuel was no longer working in California and had been working in Utah for quite some time. He had decided that he wanted me to have my baby delivered by a midwife from Utah—one our polygamist group had found. She belonged to another polygamist group, but many of our women were having their babies with her and had said she was a very good midwife.

I loved the United States and the idea of having my baby there was soothing. I knew I would be close to a hospital, unlike Mexico—and I was extremely happy at the mere thought of being away from Stella. It would be a new and wonderful experience, and I was looking forward to a life free of her and all the drama that came with her. Not that I would be there long, but even a small break from Stella was a break I desperately needed.

Samuel and I made the sixteen-hour trip, along with our two boys, in his small pickup truck. The boys rode in the front with us, which was nice because there were no connecting windows between the camper and the cab, and I would have worried about their safety had they been in the back. Because the truck had no air conditioning the heat felt unbearable at times, but as long as we kept the windows down and were traveling at a high speed, we were able to withstand it.

I had traveled to the United States many times with Samuel during our marriage—and every time we crossed the border, I would breathe a sigh of relief. I felt at home there and could almost smell the freedom that America was founded on. It spoke to something deep inside my soul and I immediately felt as light as a feather—a feather that belonged on the wing of a white bird, one that had the freedom to fly anywhere it wanted. It could flip, dip and turn any way that suited its fancy without ever worrying about going to hell for following its own intuition.

I loved the feeling of being on this side of the border. All my life I had been taught that the Bible was referencing the United States when it spoke of Sodom and Gomorrah. I was taught that it was the evil land that God would soon destroy... So I must be evil, I secretly mused, because I love the evil United States and I've never felt excited about crossing back over to the Mexican side, like Samuel always did. But that thought was just one more thing to feel guilty about and I knew I needed to get past it—my wicked, evil love for a wicked, evil country!

As we got closer to the border, and with the boys both sleeping, I found myself sinking deeper and deeper into my thoughts about my life. In the privacy of my own mind, I imagined myself making a list of all the things I felt guilty about—starting with my guilt for loving the United States, then adding the guilt I felt for being a woman, for not being Amy, and for Samuel and Stella not loving me. I also listed my many shameful acts, such as having personal needs, having feelings, and the deep shame I felt for letting God down.

As I continued making my list, I realized that I felt guilty about everything, even the simple fact that I was taking up space in the truck and breathing in the stifling air—air that should probably be reserved for my husband. And with that thought, the feelings of guilt and shame suddenly became so overwhelming that I felt like I was going to die right there in that truck—my unborn child dying right along with me.

My mind struggled to find relief from such a horrible thought and, not knowing what else to do, I decided to make a list of all the things that made me feel proud... The first thing that came to mind was the pride I felt in being a mother to Amy's children, as well as my own. But that was it. The first thing on the new list was also the last thing. And as hard as I tried to come up with at least one more thing—I couldn't. There just wasn't anything else to feel proud about.

The difference in the length of my two lists was shocking, and it was very apparent to me that there was something drastically wrong with my life! I wasn't quite sure what was wrong with it, or how it came to be that way, but it did help me understand my deep feelings of sadness.

The experience of that shocking realization was scary and at the same time, curiously interesting. Ever since I had sensed that my unborn child was a girl, something inside me had shifted. Maybe my love of being a mother and my desire to be a good mother to my daughter had given me the courage to start asking myself some questions, and at least consider the answers my heart knew to be true!

Not completely aware of it at the time, I believe it was my unborn daughter who sent me on a quest to better understand myself as a woman, perhaps so I might better understand her as a girl. A girl who deserved to be loved and cherished and valued—and made to feel important, not just as a future wife and mother, but as a person. My need to protect her from the life I was living, suddenly burst wide-open—and with that burst came two lists, one very different from the other.

I knew that I needed to face my feelings—and embrace them. Even if I had to do it secretly, I was determined not to let my daughter down. She was loved; she was cherished; she was valued; she was important—and she wasn't even born yet! To think anything else would be the greatest harm I could do to her, and I wasn't about to ever let her believe that she was less than she really was. Which, of course, meant that I also needed to believe it about myself.

We arrived in Utah the following day. A cheap, two-bedroom apartment my brother had rented for his construction workers would be our home while we were there. Samuel was working for him at the time, so he allowed us to stay there along with a few of his other workers.

By now most of the men from our church were working in the United States and leaving their wives and families in Mexico—with the excuse that it was only temporary. It seemed that the word *temporary* was a convenient way to disregard what the prophet had said about not going back over "the old trail" to the United States— temporarily convenient enough for the men who put paychecks before prophets, but not permanently convenient enough for them to give up on keeping a slew of wives in another country!

It was July 15th and my baby was due in four days. So, after taking time to settle into our apartment, I met with the midwife for a checkup and to make all the arrangements for the birth. She was a small woman who looked to be in her early sixties, with short, wavy auburn hair. Her kind eyes and gentle smile reminded me so much of Mama Vee, and I was surprised at the amount of love and support I felt from her. For the first time in a long time I felt that I had someone in my corner—someone who gave women the attention and respect they deserved. She gave me a list of supplies I needed to buy for the birth and after my visit with her, I stopped at the closest store and purchased the items on the list before going back to the apartment.

When I arrived, I found that Samuel was home and on the phone with Stella—which was certainly nothing unusual. Not bothering him, I walked into the small kitchen and began preparing supper. When he finished his conversation, he came into the kitchen where I was busy cutting up vegetables and browning rice. Without asking me anything about my visit with the midwife, he blurted out, "When exactly is this baby due?"

I had already told him (more than once), and I didn't understand the reason for his demanding question, but I answered, "On the nineteenth."

"Stella thought you were due yesterday. Somehow, I must have gotten the date wrong and told her you were due then."

I was a little confused about why it even mattered, until he added, "She's riding up to Denver from Mexico for a wedding, and she's pressuring me to come be with her. She thought you would have had your baby by now and figured I could take you home, then drive back to Denver for the wedding—then bring her back here for a turn with me. She's upset that you haven't had your baby yet, and she's worried that I'll miss the wedding."

How ridiculous, I thought. I can't control when I go into labor. Just because she wants the dates to line up perfectly for her sake doesn't mean I can make it happen. I didn't like how her ludicrous request made me feel—her pressuring me to hurry up and have my baby so *she* could be happy was unbelievable! Why is it that abso-

lutely *everything* in my life revolves around Stella, I wondered—
and why does Samuel let himself be pushed around by her?

Trying not to show how side swiped I felt, I said calmly, "I told
you all along that I was due on the nineteenth."

"I know you did," he answered. "I just wish you would have it a
few days early like you did your boys. Stella is putting me under a
lot of pressure."

You? I thought, but didn't say it… What about the pressure I'm
feeling? They were both being selfish, and it was annoying. The
whole thing was stupid—anyone with a brain should be able to figure out that babies come when they come, and not a minute sooner!
But, knowing there was nothing I could do to please either of them,
I just let it go and waited for my labor to begin. And, almost as if I
subconsciously wanted to please them both, I woke up to labor
pains the following morning.

Samuel's mother was in Utah with his sister, whose baby was
due just a few weeks after mine. So after calling the midwife to let
her know my labor had started, Samuel called his mother to let her
know as well. Although not invited, she insisted on being at my delivery so she could get a feel for how good the midwife would be
for her daughter's delivery.

Hoping it wasn't what I thought it was, I heard Samuel say, "Of
course you can be here, Mom."

The inevitable was about to intrude and before it arrived, I knew
it was coming. I absolutely did not want her at my delivery. She had
meddled so much in our family and had already caused irreparable
damage, making the friction between Stella and I needlessly worse.
I was still feeling the sharp pangs of her last meddlesome intrusion
and I didn't feel comfortable with her sharing the birth of my baby
with me.

My mind reeled as I remembered my trip to Alaska with Samuel,
my two boys and Amy's three children—who had always called me
Mama Vera, which meant the world to me. One afternoon, Elise

came into the room, looking for something in her suitcase. As she began pulling everything out of it, I asked her what she was looking for.

"I can't find my dollar bills, Aunt Vera," she said, pillaging through the neatly folded clothes.

"Aunt Vera?" I said—shocked. "Since when do you call me that?"

"Since Grandma Loretta talked to us this morning," she said, looking up from the suitcase and examining my face.

I tried not to let my disappointment show, but I knew she was picking up on it. She walked over to where I was sitting on the floor and wrapped her arms around my neck. "I love you Aunt Vera," she said, "but Grandma Loretta told me, Alice and Andrew that you're not our mom and that we can't call you Mama Vera anymore. She said we have to call you Aunt Vera."

Hurt beyond words, I didn't say anything as I hugged her back and began helping her search for her lost money again. Finding two one-dollar bills in the front pocket of her suitcase, I handed them to her—and, smiling, she ran out of the room.

Alone in the room again, I sat on the floor feeling totally crushed because of what Samuel's mother had done. What Amy's children called me was none of her concern. She had no idea what being called Mama Vera meant to me. Nor did she know how much my sister's children meant to me. My relationship with those three beautiful kids—along with my own—had kept me going in the worst of times. I endured whatever I had to endure because of them and *for* them. Silently seething, it occurred to me that maybe it wasn't because she didn't know—maybe it was because she *did* know and telling Amy's children not to call me Mom was her way of toppling the infrastructure that prolonged my survival in a very cruel world.

Either way, I assumed that after telling Samuel about it, he would straighten it out. But when I mentioned it to him, he did absolutely nothing. Apparently, it had started with Stella going to Loretta, who actually carried out the evil deed—and, once again, Stella had gotten what she wanted. So, no, I did not want Samuel's mother anywhere near me during the birth of my child—but how could I politely express this to Samuel?

Feeling another contraction, I forgot about Loretta—choosing instead to stay focused on my breathing. It was a strong one and when it subsided, I knew I needed all my mental strength for the delivery. My baby was much more important than meddlesome in-laws and now was not the time to be splitting my energy.

I didn't say anything to Samuel about it, and when she showed up—shortly after the midwife—I tried pretending she wasn't there. It wasn't easy—she talked non-stop, hardly taking a breath, yacking on and on about everything and everyone all through my labor.

She was curious about the midwife's polygamist group and had a lot of questions for her. But as she went on and on, there were moments when the pain was so intense that I wanted to scream her right out of the room—tell her to shut up, be a little more respectful of others or just go home. And, thank God, during my final contraction, I heard the midwife politely ask her to stop talking. As if she could sense my frustration, she said, "I don't mean to be rude, but Vera is trying to have a baby and we need to honor her and her birthing experience right now."

I glanced over at Samuel—smiling sheepishly at the midwife, as if to say, "I'm sorry about my mom and her loose tongue."

Loretta looked slightly embarrassed and didn't say another word to the midwife for the rest of the delivery.

I continued to feel uncomfortable having Samuel's mom in the room and couldn't help but compare how different it felt having her there instead of Mama Vee, who had been by my side loving and supporting me during my previous labors. She, on the other hand, sat off in the distance staring at my bottom, whispering to Samuel—which was degrading, humiliating, and downright rude. No wonder

Samuel was the way he was. Since birth, he had been bullied by one woman—then ended up marrying another who was exactly the same; neither caring about anyone other than themselves.

I had been bearing down for several minutes when finally, with one more long push, she was here! My beautiful baby girl was here! She was tiny with golden hair and blue eyes. Her little hands and feet were so small, but looked just like mine... A rush of emotion ran through me as she was placed in my arms and I held her against my breast. She was perfect—and the desire to protect her hit me so strongly it almost took my breath away. I looked down at her as she instinctively latched on to my breast... This little girl is perfect, I thought. And I will never allow anyone to tell her she is not.

Holding my daughter close, the feeling of total love and acceptance flowing between us was somehow combined with a glimpse of the possibility of total love and acceptance that God might have toward his little girl... Me! This feeling was powerful. So powerful that I didn't need to understand it to believe it. It was just there—and the possibility of it being true for both of us was enormous!

I loved my sons infinitely, but my daughter's birth had shown me a glimpse of God's infinite love for me. It was just a glimpse— but somehow, I knew that if I was courageous enough to stay true to myself, I would be able to see and feel God's love for me every minute of every day. Samuel didn't have much interest in choosing a name for our daughter and allowed me to name her Tia Marie. It was a name I proudly picked out; and, for the first time, I felt like I had a say about something in my life.

Now that my baby had been born, I had four days before the dreaded trip back to Mexico. After the third day I found myself still feeling extremely tired and weak. My milk had finally come in, helping soothe Tia's fussiness—which was caused by her hunger—

but I wasn't resting much while taking care of my two boys and my newborn.

My hands were full with the three of them and I wasn't recovering as fast as I had with my boys. Not only did I not feel physically ready to make the trip back to Mexico—but mentally, I wasn't ready either. I felt emotionally drained and just the thought of forcing myself to be strong was exhausting, so I decided to gather up my courage and ask Samuel if I could stay a few days longer—until I felt better.

It was late in the evening the day before we were supposed to leave. I laid on the bed trying to rest while I nursed my baby. The boys were watching a cartoon, so I closed my eyes for a few minutes, then heard the door open and Samuel coming in from work. After greeting the boys he asked if I was ready to leave tomorrow.

"Not really," I answered.

As if it were no big deal, he continued, "I want to let you know that my mom is going to be riding back to Mexico with us."

Too tired to comment, I wondered where in the heck he expected her to ride. His truck was a small Chevy S-10—not an inch of elbowroom for Samuel, me, and three children. And now we're going to add a very large woman to the mix?

As if he could read my thoughts, he said, "You'll ride in the middle with Tia on your lap and my mother will ride in the passenger seat. The boys can ride in the back. They'll be fine."

I couldn't understand how he expected me to ride between him and his mother with a stick-shift between my legs and a newborn baby on my lap for nearly two days. I had been dreading this trip, but now I was really dreading it. If I could just have a few more days for the cramping and bleeding to stop and for my milk to adjust its production, I would be able to handle it—or, at the very least, endure it. But apparently, I wasn't going to get a few more days.

A part of me was trying to convince myself that I was being a baby as I struggled to gather up the courage to ask Samuel to let me stay a few more days. But neither the courage-gathering or the asking happened. Grabbing a change of clothes from the shelf in the closet, Samuel went into the bathroom to shower while I continued nursing Tia.

Having a few more minutes to come up with a way to tell him what I needed to tell him, I used his shower-time to convince myself that I needed to be brave. To speak up. To let him know, for once, what I needed from him—instead of giving in to what he needed from me. Just a few more days was so important to me, and I believed that if I could make sure he understood how weak and tired I was, he would let me stay. My body was telling me, along with my heart, that I needed a little more time to heal. And I needed to listen to what my body and heart were saying—so, when he walked back into the room and sat at the end of the bed, I took a deep breath, summoning the courage to speak up.

My back was turned to him, which gave me a false sense of protection against the fear I was feeling. But it was either say it now, or not at all. So, almost gingerly, I said, "I need to ask a favor of you."

I said it as if I really did consider it a favor—not something I was entitled to—hoping it would be better received that way. Then I added, "Can I please stay here a few more days until I feel better? You can leave me here while you go to the wedding in Denver with Stella."

Before I could finish saying what I was determined to say, he interrupted me by saying, "Absolutely not. That is not going to happen."

"Please, Samuel," I begged. "I really don't feel good and I don't think I can handle making a long trip yet. Please." Then, hoping and praying he would understand, I offered him a few more pleading words, "By the time you get back from Denver, I'll be feeling so much better. And you don't need to call me while you're with Stella. Please, Samuel, let me stay."

I watched him shake his head as he adamantly re-stated, "It's not going to happen."

Tia had fallen asleep, and after removing my breast from her mouth, I turned to face him. I needed him to see my desperation and to realize that this might not be a big deal to him, but it was a very big deal to me. Looking at him, I continued to beg, "I know my turn is over but please, Samuel, I just need a little more time. Tia is only four days old. Sitting upright and squished between you and your mom with our daughter on my lap for two days feels impossible to me right now."

I looked into his eyes trying to find that part of him that would show some compassion for me. But he just shook his head again, saying, "Nope, we're leaving tomorrow." Then, as though I had not said a word, he turned away from me.

Once again, I heard that voice inside my head say, "See, Vera, you're just being a baby!"

But suddenly I heard myself say back to that voice, "No one is being a baby here! If this is important to you, then it is important! If it matters to you, then it matters, and that is worth noting!"

Silent as the conversation between my mind and heart was, I was surprised to hear myself defend my feelings. I quickly recognized this new voice as the part of myself that I had felt when Tia was first placed in my arms. It was a voice that was defending me against my own self-criticism and it made me think twice about the way I was thinking. It was as if it was here to save me from the hell I had been living, the hell I had allowed to take over my life—and this new voice just wasn't going there!

I did what Samuel wanted and made the trip to Mexico. I had no other choice. Sitting upright between two large bodies with my baby on my lap and my legs awkwardly spread apart so that Samuel could access the stick-shift was miserable. My lower back began cramping as though I were in labor all over again. Trying to nurse, burp or change Tia's diaper was a nightmare; and the constant nudges and bumps from either Samuel or his mother's thick arms always seemed to come at just the wrong moment.

Samuel having access to the stick-shift was obviously more important than what I had going on with the baby, so any naps were constantly interrupted. I felt miserable. The boys were in the back and would signal through the rearview mirror when they needed something, but I had no idea what they were trying to say and all I could do was watch them cry. I was sure that they either needed to eat or pee, but I had to trust that little Matthew would figure it out.

A couple of times, with Tia laying on my chest, I tried to lean my head back and sleep. But the nonstop talking and gossiping that went back and forth between Samuel and his chatterbox mom made sleeping impossible. Each time we stopped, which wasn't often, it felt like Heaven and I could hardly wait for our next stop. Being confined in one position for so many hours, along with the bumpy ride made my lower back and stomach feel like one solid boulder of pain. I could feel myself gushing blood, and I knew I shouldn't have lifted my boys out of the camper earlier in the day—but they were having a hard time, too, and they needed to know how much they were loved. I wondered how my uterus was ever going to shrink back to size if I didn't rest. My health was important to me and it bothered me that I couldn't look after myself properly, but I felt like I had no choice. Anger and resentment toward Samuel were welling up inside me. He had put me in a hopeless position—to say nothing of dangerous—but I knew better than to say anything about it. It would only land on deaf ears.

After stopping, Samuel and his mother got out of the truck. She darted to the service station bathroom as Samuel stretched his limbs and yawned. I had laid Tia on a pillow in my lap and as I gently lifted the pillow up, I could see that I was saturated with blood. It was running down the insides of my legs. I knew this was too much blood, caused by doing too much too soon. Carefully, and trying not to panic, I placed Tia on the front seat of the truck, then I slowly got out and walked to the back to let the boys out and to get some clean clothes to change into. Although the toys from the McDonald's Happy Meals had been keeping them entertained, they were both happy to get out and walk around a little.

After Samuel took his turn using the bathroom, he kept an eye on the boys while he gassed up the truck. Meanwhile, I took Tia with me into the bathroom to change us both. I laid her on the changing station and quickly began removing my soiled clothes. The amount of blood scared me. As I stepped out of my bloody garments, along with three saturated pads, I noticed a piece of my heart growing cold.

I began to cry uncontrollably as I felt myself surrendering. The realization that all I had been living and doing to gain Samuel's love, and therefore God's love, was not enough and never would be… Staying in Utah for a few more days would have meant the world to me, but it meant absolutely nothing to Samuel. I knew he didn't care, and suddenly neither did I.

I don't want to try anymore, my heart sobbed. I don't care if I go to hell and never make it to Heaven! If I have to spend one more day disconnected from myself to survive this pathway to Heaven, then I don't want Heaven! Not only is it killing me, it's not even working! I'm still not good enough and I truly have given it my all—God knows I've given it my all! Since the day I was born, I've been living my life the way Dad taught me to so I could make it to Heaven. But it's not enough.

The pain in my heart from ignoring my own feelings for so long was no longer deniable. It came pouring through me as I realized that I would never be accepted by the two most dominant men in my life: Dad and Samuel. The pain in my heart was a million times worse than the pain in my back and my stomach—and, suddenly, I let it go.

"I don't care about the gospel! I don't care about the Mormon leaders! I don't care about making it to Heaven or to hell! I don't care!" I cried out loud, splashing water onto my face.

Emotionally spent, I finished cleaning myself up *and* the mess in the bathroom. I dried my face, then stood beside my sleeping daughter—watching her. She was so beautiful—her little chest rising and falling as she breathed in and out. I suddenly imagined myself as God, and Tia as me... What a beautiful creation I have created, I heard myself saying to her—so perfect, so innocent and pure. That is what you are, I said—as God. So why do you believe you have to jump through hoops to be in my presence? Don't you know, my little darling, that just being you is enough?

And there it was again! A part of me, showing myself a glimpse of who I really am!

Tia began to stir, and I picked her up and held her close to my heart. Although it was my baby girl I was holding, I imagined I was holding myself—as a baby. I could feel the love and nurturing I had always longed for. And as I stood once again in front of the sink, I looked into the mirror—into my own eyes—and made a promise to myself. The girl staring back at me looked so sad and as I looked deep into her eyes, I whispered these words, "From now on, I promise to listen to you. I promise to spend time getting to know you. I promise to honor and love you, but most important of all, I promise to let you shine. I promise."

Smiling as I whispered the last words of my promise, the girl in the mirror smiled back.

CHAPTER TWENTY-FIVE

I'LL TAKE THE ONE PERCENT

If you want to begin a spiritual journey, just clean out a closet. When you physically get rid of what no longer serves you in your outer-world, it inspires you to start looking for what no longer serves you in your inner-world. Which, in turn, inspires you to clean out another closet.

It has been five months since Tia's birth. I hadn't completely stopped bleeding yet, but I refused to see a doctor, even though Samuel had suggested it. Assuming my body needed extra healing time—after that miserable two-day trip—I wasn't alarmed. Besides, it was a good reason for Samuel to stay away from me sexually. So many changes had been going on inside my head and within my heart, and I wasn't ready to deal with that part of my marital duties yet. So, extra healing time was fine with me.

More cooking, cleaning and washing for Samuel and my children, along with nurturing Amy's children, yard work and community events seemed to take up most of my time. I had been trying to identify with more of my feelings but found myself just going through the motions of my life most of the time. I no longer felt the need or the desire to bend over backwards to make it to

Heaven. I felt like I was in limbo, and I was enjoying how it felt not to care.

I knew that not caring and not trying could very possibly lead me straight to hell, but I still didn't care. Going to hell sounded so much easier than jumping through all the hoops I had been jumping through in hopes of being somewhat worthy of Heaven, so I spent my days loving my children and my sister's children as a few more years slipped by.

During those years, I noticed that I was more hopeful than I had been before, although nothing about my life or my circumstances had really changed. It felt like something wonderful was brewing in the back of my mind and heart, and that it was going to come forward when the timing was right.

There is a great calmness that comes with acceptance while still embracing hope, and I continued to be the dutiful wife and sister wife without it being as emotionally charged as it had been before. Instead of sinking into the middle of all the polygamist drama, I simply observed the heavy requirements that were put upon me and all other female members from our church in a different light. Although I didn't quite have the strength to stand up against it yet, I was noticing it and paying attention to how abusive and sexist it all was.

Watching my children grow had brought me so much joy and I constantly thanked God for them in my prayers. Yes, I was still praying, but the God I was praying to had changed in small but important ways. I was still afraid of him, but whatever that wonderful thing was that was brewing in the back of my mind, it had softened this new God a little. Just a little, which I found interesting.

Matthew and Bobby had started school and their developing personalities were beginning to show. It intrigued me to see how two little boys, raised by the same parent and under the same circumstances, could be so different... Matthew loved to garden and to build things. He loved school and was very responsible about doing his homework. Bobby despised school and couldn't wait to get home to play with his friends. He would take everything to heart and give everything he had away. He also loved going to work with his dad, whereas Matthew preferred to do things on his own. They were so different from one another, and it piqued my interest in psychology and the workings of the mind.

Little Tia had become quite tough having two older brothers to defend herself against. I admired her ability to voice her thoughts. I didn't want her to grow up being brainwashed and someday be forced into submission by one of our polygamist men, so I repeatedly encouraged her to stand up for herself. She was now five—very smart for her age—and she made me smile every day with her inquisitive mind. In many ways, she reminded me of myself.

Andrew, Alice and Elise were all teenagers now. My relationship and special connection with them opened my eyes to the special connection I felt with all children—especially teenagers. I seemed to have a natural ability to make them feel like they could be themselves around me, making it easier for them to talk to me about their struggles. I loved helping them feel understood and loved—giving them what I so desperately wanted and needed myself: Love and acceptance.

Tia had started preschool, and with her gone in the mornings along with the boys, I found myself taking time to dig deeper into myself—what I really believed, what I truly felt, what I wanted to hold onto, and what I was struggling to let go of… The moment I decided that I no longer wanted to try to be and do all the things required of me to be accepted into Heaven, or to earn myself a place on Dad's worthy-list or in Samuel's heart, was the beginning of my spiritual awakening. I found myself reading through all the Mormon scriptures, Jerome's teachings, the King James version of the Bible and anything else I could get my hands on. I longed to understand my life and to understand the God who every man in my small world believed in. I wanted to see for myself if these books spoke to me the way Dad claimed they spoke to him, and the way Samuel claimed they spoke to him, and the way all the women in our church, including myself, had accepted—even though it was close to unbearable for most of us.

I had once overheard Samuel having a conversation with a born-again Christian. He was trying to convince this individual that Jerome's way was the right way, and he said something that I will never forget—that the Scriptures were only true if they were translated correctly. Of course Samuel and our church members believed we had the only true translation. But I took what he said and gave it a totally different meaning for myself. To me it meant that I had the right—woman or not—to read the Scriptures and to translate them to mean whatever the spirit of God led me to understand in that moment. That was such a liberating thought. It meant that I could trust my own guidance.

One morning, after my children had left for school, I got busy doing my household chores and decided the coat closet needed cleaning. Sorting through old, outgrown coats and jackets, I noticed how messy the shelves in the back of the closet were. I had stashed a few board games there but mostly books, which I'd found at garage sales whenever I was in the States—but hadn't read. So, after organizing shoes, skates, and whatever outerwear still fit my children, I started going through the books. One in particular caught my eye—a book called *A Return to Love* by Marianne Williamson. I had never heard of her, but I remembered buying the book simply because of the picture of her on the cover, along with a word I had yearned to understand all my life—the word Love.

I turned it over and read the back cover then set it aside, intending to read the whole book as soon as I had some quiet time. The next few books I picked up were the *Book of Mormon* along with *The Saunders Story*, *Pearl of Great Price*, and the *Doctrine and Covenants*—mostly Mormon scriptures, considered our scriptures as well. I was very familiar with these books because they were the foundation of my entire life. Mom and Dad had countless sets of these books around the house and as an indoctrinated mother and wife myself, I also had copies of them. As I sorted through them, out of nowhere, feelings of anger and resentment plowed through me. The words and beliefs these books contained had brought me so much suffering, and I suddenly hated them. Caught up in a whirlwind of raw emotion, I threw them across the room—feeling a rush of adrenaline course through my veins as they hit the floor. And then came the shame.

As I stood staring at the books scattered across the floor, the voice inside my head exploded with a vengeance, reprimanding me for my flagrant disrespect of God's words. How dare you, it screamed. How dare you! Then came the voice inside my heart— fighting for its life—demanding to know why I was expected to live outside my heart and soul in order to keep God's word.

Leave me alone, my heart begged... You have taken me nowhere for years. These Scriptures speak of nothing but guilt and fear, and I can't listen to it anymore! I have lived my life, bound to a God whose holy *men* have damn near killed me! I feel broken because I've neglected my true self by listening to you, and I will not allow you to destroy me!

More waves of anger raged through me as I stared at the supposedly holy books. I wanted to stomp on them, rip them to shreds and set them on fire. But, suddenly, my anger turned to sorrow, and I began to weep.

Falling to my knees, I sobbed like a broken child... Years of pent-up emotions flowed through my eyes, disguised as tears. Waves of pain and heartache and abuse—the only things I ever believed I was worthy of—released themselves, sob after sob, until my throat was so sore I could barely swallow.

All cried out, I finally picked myself up off the floor—surprised by how much lighter I felt. Slowly, I walked over to the books I had hurled across the room and picked each one of them up. A part of me wanted to throw them in the garbage, but I couldn't because they were so closely connected with Dad, my marriage, and my current life. Even though I desperately wanted to let go of it all, I just wasn't ready to do it yet. I didn't know who I was without my religious beliefs—and I knew I needed to know before I let them go. I wasn't strong enough or brave enough to stand up for myself yet and just the thought of facing Dad and Samuel with my opposing point of view terrified me, so I decided to put the books in a garbage bag and store them in the back of the closet for a while longer. I would only keep them there for security, I told myself, while I went about getting mentally and emotionally stronger.

And so, a beautiful journey of self-discovery began. Beautiful because of where it led me, not because it lacked hardship. It took a tremendous amount of courage to peel back the layers of my beliefs—one by one—and to form new beliefs based on my own internal guidance system. I could feel myself going against the grain of the thoughts and beliefs of all the people surrounding me; and as I observed my life from a new perspective, it got harder and harder to go along with being submissive and to engage in my own polygamist reality.

I soon went through a stage where, no matter how much I read, I just couldn't read enough. I drank up new spiritual ideas as if they were holy water, and I could hardly wait for my alone time in the mornings to explore new ideas and philosophies that challenged my old beliefs.

What I found myself doing when studying or reading someone else's perspective on life was to stay open to new ideas without judgment. It didn't mean that I had to take every word that was written and make it gospel or even believe it for that matter. It just meant that I listened to my heart when hearing or reading it, and I trusted what felt true to me. It took me a while to acquire the skill of listening to my own inner-voice and to trust that voice, but with patience I got better and better at it.

On one of these mornings, I vividly recalled a conversation I'd had with Samuel about Jerome and God's prophets. Samuel had quoted from Scripture that if a man teaches ninety-nine truths and one false truth, we are to consider him a false prophet. He adamantly believed that Jerome was the only man on the face of the earth that had spoken one hundred percent truth and, therefore, he was the only true prophet. Samuel insisted that we could not trust the words of anyone else because they were laden with half-truths—making them wrong. But as I dared to read and listen to others, I realized that it was up to me to choose what the whispering of the spirit (as they say in Mormonism) guided me to believe as truth.

And, on my new quest to discover my *own* truth, I began to find truth everywhere! And the more open I was and the more willing I was to listen to my own soul, the more truth I found. The truth about innocence, I found in a baby's smile; and the truth about love was in the eyes of a beggar when she came knocking at my door asking me for a few pesos. It didn't take long for me to notice that whenever I stayed open to my own truth, the real truth about God kept showing itself to me.

As I continued to read different spiritual books, I wondered if the *opposite* of what Samuel had quoted might be true. What if ninety-nine percent of what I was reading was false and only one percent of it was true?

Then I'll take the one percent that speaks truth to me, I decided, and leave the rest on the page for the next reader to find their own truth.

CHAPTER TWENTY-SIX

LITTLE UNWORTHY ME

Here I am, on the path to Heaven, not worth more than the old rag used to wash the kitchen floor... That is the value of a polygamist wife—well, maybe I'm not being totally honest. Because, truthfully, the old rag is worth a dime—and I'm only worth a penny.

One cloudy morning I was doing my morning chores—washing dishes, sweeping and mopping the floors along with washing a few loads of laundry. But when I went outside to hang the clothes on the clothesline, it began to rain—so I went back into the house and decided to wait for the storm to clear up before hanging the clothes out to dry.

I had three hours to myself before the children would be home so, grabbing a blanket along with a cup of tea and Marianne Williamson's book—which I hadn't gotten to yet—I sat down on the couch, excited about reading *A Return to Love*.

As I began to read, everything seemed to be speaking to me and I found myself immersed in a world of all-inclusive love that was so real and so divine that every time I turned a page, I felt more and more alive! I absorbed every word, letting each one float through my soul, lift me up and carry me to a place where I was understood, valuable, and loved. Pausing for a sip of tea, I noticed that it had gotten cold, so I glanced at the clock—shocked that what seemed to have been no more than a few minutes of quiet reading time had actually been two hours!

I didn't want to put the book down and instead of jumping up to get a few more chores done, I simply put my feet up on the couch and laid back—book still in my hands; my soul ready for more... I continued reading until I came to the chapter titled "You." This chapter explained how God loves us all—you *and* me, no matter who we are. And, for the first time in my life, I actually felt the reality of God *really* loving me. Completely amazed by the feeling, I gently placed the open book down on my chest, allowing the feeling of being loved by God to penetrate my whole being.

"God loves me," I said out loud. "Me! Little unworthy me!"

I could feel the trueness of the truth washing over me, encircling me, becoming part of me—the intensity of it bringing me to tears... Starting at the top of my head, it worked its way all the way down to my feet, then back up into my heart and chest area where it pulsated with rhythmic vibrancy. As I surrendered to it, I could feel myself enveloped in its warmth which brought more tears to my eyes as I looked up—feeling the expansiveness of the Universe, the expansiveness of God's love for me.

The tears wouldn't stop, but they were happy tears and I couldn't help but smile while I was crying. "Yes, God, I accept your love. And not only do I accept it, God, I can feel it," I whispered.

I closed my eyes and basked in the feeling of this love and, suddenly, a feeling of freedom came over me and I caught a glimpse of a white bird—so white it was almost blue. I had the sensation of it flying from my left shoulder into the sky and out into the Universe... I was left with the most beautiful feeling of peace and as I opened my eyes again, I uttered the words, "Thank you, God. Thank you for loving me—little unworthy me."

Feeling loved by God and free to keep learning whatever I wanted to learn, my hunger for knowledge and understanding grew stronger every day—and with it came a desire to understand the human body. How we are made up of trillions of cells, each playing a role in our wholeness, intrigued me. The functioning of the internal organs, the brain, our cells and the capacity of the body to create more of them was fascinating to me.

Included in my quest for knowledge, I had been studying a book on the female reproductive system. I read this book from start to finish and reread the chapter on ovulation. After having my experience with the whitish-blue bird, I could sense freedom somewhere in my future and I felt an urgency to understand the reproductive rhythm of my own body so I could protect myself from getting pregnant again—which would make it harder for my freedom to be attained.

The form of birth control talked about in this book was called "rhythm." It was not a very effective way to stop unwanted pregnancies due to unpredictable menstrual cycles causing the unpredictability of ovulation unless, of course, you were determined to figure out a way to make it work. And I was determined—*very* determined. So I opened the book once again to the page that had an ovulation chart on it.

Because I couldn't predict my next period cycle, I took my longest cycle and my shortest cycle and combined them both to make a single chart that I paid very close attention to. This worked like a charm—but would only continue to work like a charm if I continued to keep Samuel away from me during the times I knew I could get pregnant. Paying attention to the fertility rhythms of my body was also helping me pay more attention to my overall well-being and to my feelings.

Samuel seemed to be unaware of the changes that were taking place within me and noticed only that I wasn't getting pregnant. On one occasion he drove me into town himself to take me to see the doctor to find out why. I was not about to tell him the reason why, so I went along with his plan. I visited the doctor while Samuel waited in the waiting room. I answered all the doctor's questions and after his diagnosis of presumed hormonal imbalance, he prescribed some medication for me. We left the clinic and drove straight to a pharmacy. I waited outside in the car while Samuel went inside to pick up the medication. He came out a few minutes later and handed me a box of pills. "Make sure you take these," was all he said.

I nodded my head, knowing nothing was wrong with me and that I didn't need medication. But a nod can mean a lot of things—and I didn't take a single one of those pills. I just stuck with my chart and continued practicing the rhythm-method.

I had to continue to find excuses for not allowing him to have sex with me, and I used the excuse of not feeling well or having a headache a lot. But the one that worked the best was, "I'm on my period." In the past, I would have struggled with telling these little white lies, but I knew in my heart that the loving God I had found understood my reasoning and the soon-to-be freedom that I was trying to protect.

Perhaps the right thing to do would have been to tell Samuel what I was thinking and about the changes I was experiencing—to share the truth with him, and say calmly, "No you can't have sex with me because I don't want to get pregnant. I sense that I'm going to be leaving you soon and more children will make it difficult for me to do so."

Yes, maybe that would have been better, but the thought of telling him I had no intention of staying with him sent sheer panic through my whole body. It wasn't the right time. I wasn't ready. I didn't even want to bring it up until I knew I could not be talked out of it—or guilted out of it or shamed out of it. And, at this point, I wasn't quite there. I couldn't possibly tell Samuel yet, and I certainly wasn't ready to tell Dad. Just the thought of it scared the daylights out of me—so much so that I even considered just waiting for him to die. Then I would flee.

Time slipped by rather quickly as my appetite for spiritual under-standing became insatiable. I secretly began to study various religions and, as I gained insight into different beliefs, I realized that all religions teach some form of truth. A truth that may or may not be true but silenced many unanswerable questions.

I continued my studies of the human brain and Abraham Maslow's studies of the Hierarchy of Needs. I found it all so fasci-nating, and it filled up my alone time—which I had grown to love. Just me, a cup of tea, and a stack of books—constantly reminding myself that all would be well if I paid close attention to the rhythm chart.

I also began to get more involved with the youth in our commu-nity. I taught two separate youth classes using the church's material to teach, but always making sure that love was the focal point of my lessons. Especially Self-Love. My students felt comfortable around me, and it gave me the opportunity to open their minds a little as I gained mental strength myself. I longed for those adolescents to think for themselves and to realize they had choices—but I wanted to be allowed to keep teaching them, so I was very careful about how I delivered this message.

One day, when I had just finished up with one of my classes and was walking out to my car, I noticed Mama Vee driving up the road. She stopped, rolled the window down, and smiled her usual big smile. I walked over to her and after visiting for a few minutes, she told me Dad had been struggling with a very bad case of the flu. She said he wasn't doing too well, so I told her I would stop in to visit him before going home.

I felt slightly obligated. Being around him still scared me, even though in the back of my heart I prayed I would someday feel differently, wishing I loved him more than I feared him. After all, I thought, he's my father and daughters surely must love their fathers.

After driving the few blocks to Mama Vee's, I took a deep breath, then walked up to her house and through the front door. Dad was in the back room resting on the bed and I sat on a chair next to him. I wanted him to know the reason for my visit was because I cared, but I was so nervous—my old friend, Fear, growing bigger by the minute.

I knew the new belief system I was creating for myself went against everything Dad believed in and had taught me; and I felt like a rebellious child sitting there next to him—my beliefs secretly clashing with his. Every wife and child in our polygamist family knew there were consequences for clashing with his beliefs, which made me incredibly nervous because I was afraid that just by looking at me, he would know that I no longer agreed, accepted or believed in his vengeful God—a God who made women lesser than men, a God who threatened us with hell if we did not follow the rules, a God who taught not love but fear. I tried to overcome my nervousness, calming myself a bit by remembering why I was there—to show my father that I cared about him, *not* to share my secret with him.

Dad opened his eyes and smiled at me. I smiled back and asked him how he was feeling.

His smile was quickly replaced with a look of disdain. "Not worth a darn, sister. This flu really got me this time," he said, as he began to cough.

I could hear the phlegm loosening in his throat as he coughed a few more times, then blew his nose, and finally settled back in the bed.

"You know, I'm not going to be around much longer," he said, rubbing his hand over his bald head.

He had been saying for years that he was going to die when he reached the age his father was when he died—which he had now surpassed by a few years. Listening to him made me smile on the inside. This was not the first time he thought he was on his death-bed, and I had a feeling he was tired of living.

With the new perspective I was gaining, I could see that for him to be so hard on me, he would have to be extremely hard on him-self—and it seemed like his chosen lifestyle had begun to take a toll on him. This realization didn't ease my fear of him though, and the mere thought of ever standing up to him still felt frightening and impossible.

Almost as if he had read my thoughts he said, "You know, sister, I'm glad you came to visit me. I've wanted to talk to you about something very important that's been on my mind."

He proceeded without caution or compassion—comparing me to my sister, Cheryl, and rambling on about how she didn't have an evil bone in her body.

I had to look down and swallow hard a few times to stop myself from laughing out loud. You don't know Cheryl at all, I thought. She has a lot more bad feelings about you, polygamy and this reli-gion than I've ever had!

He continued talking, letting me know that I needed to wake up every morning and try to be more like her. Why? Because she's bet-ter than me at putting a smile on her face to cover up her pain and misery... You don't have a clue, I thought, as the humor I had felt about what he was saying began to turn into anger.

He went on, "You're just a little spitfire, and if you're ever going to make it into Heaven, you need to be more submissive."

A spitfire? More submissive? What in the heck do you want from me, Dad? I have bent over backwards for you, for your God and for your religion. I gave my life away in search of your love and your God's love; and after all these years of being obedient and submissive, I'm still not enough.

I wanted to scream at him. I wanted to tell him how he had bro-ken my spirit and how I had spent years keeping it broken so he and

his God might love me and might allow me into their kingdom…
Yeah, right, I need to be more like Cheryl. Go to hell, Dad! Just as I
have given up on pleasing Samuel, I am now giving up on pleasing
you! I may still be afraid of you, of your God and of what being a
spitfire may mean to both of you, but *my* God loves me—spitfire
and all! And yes, I will continue to wake every morning, just as you
suggested, but *not* trying to be anything or anyone other than me!

Although I didn't say any of this out loud to him, I said it to myself and that was enough to stop the mental agony I normally
bought into. I no longer believed any of it—it was all nonsense.

CHAPTER TWENTY-SEVEN

FREE TO FLY

One wing or two, if you're going with the wind instead of against it, you will use what you've got and somehow you'll glide beyond the stars.

The following day, I attended a baby shower for a young woman from our church that was being held in the backyard of her mother's home. Arriving a few minutes late, I placed my gift on the gift table, then made my way over to the women waiting in line for their turn at the taco salad bar.

After serving myself, I sat down with a group of women, listening to bits and pieces of their conversations with each other. Talk about so and so's husband, somebody's sister wife, last Sunday's meeting topic and some light-minded chatter swirled around me. As I listened and watched these women, I suddenly realized that I no longer fit in. I felt like an outsider and, as I watched them, I was shocked at what I could see so clearly now. What they all had in common was the story in their eyes—eyes filled with loneliness, unworthiness, longing, and suffering; all the feelings that used to haunt my soul with every breath I took.

I knew I had been changing, but it was in those few moments that I realized just how much. I felt like a foreigner amongst the

women I had known for so long and it was, to say the least, uncomfortable—so, without a word, I quietly left the party.

I slowly walked home by myself, feeling as though I had become
someone different without realizing just how different I had become. Everyone and everything around me felt familiar, and yet it
was not. No matter what I looked at, it seemed as though I was seeing it for the first time—the dirt roads, the ditches and all the houses
I had passed a thousand times, somehow looked very different to
me.

I felt as though I had been living a fog-covered life for a very
long time—struggling inside a gloomy, stifling, dirty mist where the
air felt thick and heavy. Even now, I saw and felt it as if I were an
outsider looking in, and I noticed that I had finally begun to separate
myself from it—that it was becoming more unfamiliar every day.

I will be getting the hell out of here someday, I thought, but I
don't think I can wait until after Dad dies. I need to go soon. But I
can't until I find the courage to tell him and Samuel that I'm leaving. And as that thought fired through me, I began to tremble with
fear.

As I walked through my own yard, I heard birds singing in the
trees, which brought me a comforting feeling of peace—and again, I
heard that little voice inside me saying, *You will have the courage
when the time is right, and when the time is right, you will know it.*
My fears soothed by the loving voice within me, I went into my
own home which, lately, had become my sacred place—a place
where, day by day, I was secretly changing my beliefs.

Later that evening, after my children had fallen asleep and Samuel
had left my house to spend the night with Stella, I crawled into bed
and tried to sleep. I felt so restless because of what I had felt earlier
in the day at the baby shower... Imaginary scenes of how I would
tell Dad and Samuel I was leaving ran through my mind, and I
wondered where I would go, how I would get there, how my chil-

dren would handle such a big change, and what would happen to my relationship with Amy's children. Then I wondered if my dad would despise me for leaving, if Samuel would try to keep my children from me, and what my family members—especially my brothers—would say... Am I strong enough to face the coming wrath? Am I courageous enough to leave? Will Stella finally be happy?

Questions, questions, and more questions raced through my mind—the biggest one being: What will Dad do when he finds out? I wasn't sure I wanted to know. Just the thought of what the answer might be, terrified me; and I wondered how I would ever find the courage to tell him. How would I bear his condemnation and judgment? I couldn't imagine how I could ever stand up to him and tell him I wanted to live my own life, choose my own beliefs, find my own truth, and do what felt right to me. A wave of hopelessness washed over me as I felt my dream of freedom fading into exactly what it was—just a dream!

No, I told myself, I cannot give up on myself. I must find the courage to face Dad.

I had taught my youth students that to be good at something they had to practice, and I knew this applied to me as well. Jumping out of bed, I ran into the bathroom, turned on the light, and stood in front of the mirror. I looked deep into my own eyes until I could see the light of my soul looking back at me. I smiled, and as it smiled back, it seemed to be saying, "You can do this, just practice."

Not moving, I pretended the eyes that were staring back at me were Dad's eyes, and that it was Dad's face I was looking at—not my own. I started to cry as I told Dad what was in my heart... "I'm leaving your religion and I'm leaving Samuel. I'm not Amy and I don't love him. Please understand me. I'm not trying to be disrespectful; I just don't feel the way I believe a real wife should feel about a real husband. I want out!"

Suddenly, the light I had seen in my own eyes turned to fear—which petrified me. Instead of just *pretending* my own reflection was Dad, all I could see was my *real* Dad glaring at me. Then he disappeared, replaced by a frightened little girl looking back at me. A shiver went down my spine.

I desperately wanted to hold the frightened little girl who was staring back at me from the mirror, but instead I tried to coax her into feeling better. "You'll be okay," I said out loud. "We'll keep practicing like this in the mirror every day until you're stronger. You have *got* to do this. The only way out is to push through the fear. You can do it. Together, we'll get through this."

Practicing in front of the mirror became a part of my daily morning routine. I struggled the first few times. I kept wanting to go back to the safety I felt whenever thoughts about waiting to leave until after Dad's death filled my mind. After a while though, I started getting better at it—and I noticed that I was gaining more confidence in myself. Practicing in front of the mirror was doing more than just helping me overcome my fear of standing up to Dad—it was helping me see where in my life I was strong and where I struggled with weakness. I began looking forward to my mirror-time every day—feeling better about myself every time I made even the tiniest bit of progress.

Andrew had moved away from home. He was living in the United States full-time doing construction work and dating a girl named Justine, the daughter of a polygamist man. Alice had married a nice young man and had a beautiful baby boy. Elise had been dating Justine's brother for a while and seemed to be in love. Stella had two more children after I gave birth to Tia. But more children didn't make her a better person—and, of course, she remained the same ornery sister wife she had always been... No longer having the desire to please God by living celestial marriage with her, I simply ignored her—staying devoted to my spiritual quest and to myself, only communicating with her when necessary. Samuel wasn't happy about it and often expressed frustration about the distance and lack of caring between us, but I no longer cared what he thought, and I certainly wasn't going to waste my time trying to fix it. My catering days were over—I had much more important things to do.

Early one afternoon, while I was in the kitchen putting clean dishes away, I heard someone knocking at the back door. It was a faint knock, so I knew it had to be one of Stella's children. "Come in," I hollered, as I bent down to put some pans in the lower cupboard.

Mandy, Stella's second-born daughter, smiled at me from the doorway. She had her beautiful blonde hair pulled back in a pony-tail and was wearing a cute flowered summer dress. Holding out a cup, she asked if she could borrow some sugar for her mom.

"Sure," I said, still stacking pans on the bottom shelf of the cup-board, "just give me a minute."

As she stood in the doorway waiting for me to finish, she said excitedly, "Aunt Vera, did you know that Elise is getting married to Jeremy? They just got engaged a few minutes ago!"

Elise was the last of Amy's three children to be leaving home, and I wasn't aware of the just-minutes-ago engagement. "No, I didn't know, sweetie," I answered. "Thank you for telling me," I added, closing the cupboard doors and noticing a strange yet famil-iar feeling come over me. Once again, out of nowhere, the sensation of a bird—white with a slight hue of blue—flew from my right shoulder into the atmosphere. There was no bird, of course, but the sensation was very strong—and as it enveloped me, coming from somewhere deep in my soul, I heard the words: *You're free.*

It was oddly beautiful—the feeling and the words—and I knew in that moment the time had come. My work was done, and I was free to fly!

A feeling of excitement came over me as I filled Mandy's cup with sugar. She thanked me, then went out the back door while I stood in awe of what had just happened... I'm free, I thought. I'm free!

I ran down the hallway and into my bedroom closet. I wanted to be alone with this feeling for a minute, so I closed the door. It was dark, but I didn't care as I dropped to my knees and began to talk to my God. Not to Dad's God. Not to Samuel's God. But to *my* God, the creator of my soul.

"I am so excited, but I'm scared," I said out loud. I remembered the Bible verses: *Knock and the door shall be opened.* And, *Ask and ye shall receive.* These verses had spoken truth to me in the past and they were speaking truth to me now.

"God," I continued, "I have knocked, and I have asked, and I am going to trust that you will come through for me. Please hold my hand when I tell Samuel and, please God, hold my hand when I face my father. I need you. I cannot do this on my own!"

It felt like God was speaking back to me through my thoughts... I imagined a father speaking to his daughter—a little girl who is afraid of the dark. She wants to learn how to turn the light on herself and her father knows she can do it. He also knows that if he does it for her, she will not realize her own ability to do it herself. If he does it for her, she will be in the same situation the next time a dark moment surrounds her. "I will not do this for you," he is saying, "but I will stand right here by your side as you do it. Go ahead, darling, step up on the tips of your toes and turn the light on. Daddy is right here."

I couldn't help but feel that if I were bound by real chains and locks, it would be much easier to escape. But the mental bondage I was currently facing felt so much harder to break away from. I felt emotionally trapped, and I didn't know which of the chains to break free of first—there were so many of them! But knowing that my God was with me brought me comfort and I did my best to trust that I had what it would take within me to set myself free.

At the time, I had an inkling that the battle ahead of me was mostly inside me. It related to others, indeed, but had to be overcome by my own ability to fight for myself—and for my freedom.

I will prevail, I promised myself, wiping the last of my tears away... Tears of excitement, fear and gratitude were all mixed together, but after brushing them away, I opened the closet door and sat on the foot of my bed for a few minutes. I began making mental notes of all I needed to do to prepare for my exit. And, not wanting to leave before Elise's wedding and possibly ruin her special day, I gave myself until her wedding day to prepare. Not such a big deal, considering I had already waited fourteen years. Another three months, I decided, was nothing compared to the waiting I had already done.

In the days that followed, I constantly reminded myself that I was strong, that I could do it, that I could leave Samuel and start a new life—and not only did I start putting some money away, I also mapped out a plan. I didn't know where I would be going or how I would be going but for now the most important thing for me to do was to prepare myself, not just for the journey, but for the fiery outburst I knew would be coming.

CHAPTER TWENTY-EIGHT

NO!

No one knows what will buy them their ticket to freedom. Sometimes, it's something beautiful. Other times, it's the last whimper—right before the lights go out in your soul.

It is the day after Elise's wedding. Samuel had been experiencing pain in his forearm and was having a minor surgical procedure done at the hospital. His mother and Stella drove into town with him that morning and after the procedure was over, they both drove home while Samuel stayed in the hospital to recover for a few hours.

It was now my turn to be with him, so I would be driving into town to pick him up and bring him home. Everything was always about turns and never about feelings or connecting with each other—but I was used to it and if it was my turn, then it was my turn, so I agreed to pick him up.

I finished my morning chores and had an hour before it was time for me to leave, so I sat on the couch, resting my head on the back as I closed my eyes. I recalled the events from the wedding yesterday. It was held in our backyard amongst the pecan trees. The setting was beautiful, with tables and chairs spread out under the trees. Beautiful decorations, along with white tablecloths, covered the tables. Elise looked perfect, all dressed in white—reminding me so much of her mother on the day she had married Samuel, all those years ago. That fateful day—the day that made her so happy, never dreaming that her marriage would impact so many lives, especially mine. As I thought about Amy and the part I had played in her children's upbringing, I felt a sense of pride and I knew she was as proud of me as I was of myself—I could feel it.

Although Stella fought with all her might to keep your children away from me, I silently said to Amy, I was able to help them feel loved. I promised you I would, and I believe I have succeeded. With *your* help I have succeeded. Perhaps Samuel has never recognized the role I've played in their lives, but you do, and that is all that matters.

Tilting my head back, I smiled up at her as if she were in the room with me. I imagined her smiling back and saying, "Thank you for all you have done. You are now free to live your own life. No more sacrificing... Go find happiness, my dear little sister. I love you."

"I love you too," I whispered.

I arrived at the hospital with clean clothes for Samuel to change into. I opened the door to the room where he was waiting and found him sitting on the edge of the hospital bed visiting with a male friend of his who had stopped by to say hello.

I handed him his clothes, and he made his way into the bathroom to change. I made small talk with his friend while we waited for him to return to the room. A few minutes later, dressed and ready to go, he and his friend exchanged a few more words while I bent down to tie his shoes. I was mentally and emotionally so far away from him that I felt like I was performing an act of kindness for a complete stranger.

After saying goodbye to his friend, we left the hospital and stopped at a local restaurant to eat before going home. I noticed that I felt odd, as though I were disconnected from my body. It felt like I was a few inches outside of myself—watching myself have this experience.

We each ate our meal of soup and tortillas without me uttering a word. I had absolutely nothing to say but, of course, Samuel did—commenting on how I never talked to him anymore when we were together.

It was true—I had stopped talking to him years ago, except when I absolutely had to; and I was a little surprised it had taken him this long to notice. He sat looking at me from across the table as though he were disgusted with me—as though it was my duty to talk to him.

"Say something," he finally said, as I sat in silence.

I wasn't trying to upset him. My desire to please him had disappeared long ago, leaving no reason for me to communicate with him anymore. That was it. So obvious to me, but apparently not so obvious to him.

"You know," he said harshly, "sometimes I wonder if you want a fucking divorce!"

He had never referenced divorce before, much less used that kind of language and that tone of voice with which to reference it. It completely surprised me, but before he could take it back, I heard myself answer, "I do."

I immediately felt some relief, then came a truckload of fear. I tried to brace myself for whatever consequences I had to face for letting him know that I wanted out.

He stared at me, flabbergasted. As though my answer caught him completely off guard.

"What?" he said. "I didn't really mean that. I was just trying to pressure you into talking to me."

Well, it backfired, I thought, as I said to him, "I *do* want a divorce."

He had set it up perfectly! For me, the scary part was how to *begin* the "I'm-leaving-you" conversation—once I got through that,

I was sure I could just roll right through the rest of it. Samuel had no spine, which was blatantly obvious when he was around his mother or Stella; and now that he had opened the door to the subject of divorce—without me having to do much of anything—I just followed his lead. I did it! I dared to tell him I wanted out! Not that there wouldn't be any consequences for me after he had a chance to absorb it—I knew the consequences were coming—but I was so proud of myself that I didn't think much about what might happen next.

The drive home was a silent one—the kind of silence where you just know you're in trouble. But my shackles were all emotional, binding me with fear, shame, and guilt. I knew that my new belief system was about to be tested, and I also knew this was my chance to prove to myself just how strong I really was—*and* how strong my new belief system was. I wanted my freedom. I wanted to break away from my miserable marriage, which was the only way I would ever be free from the disgusting cult I had been born into... Wow, have I changed! I even dared to think of this religion, my father's religion, as a cult.

After arriving home, Samuel parked the car in my driveway and walked over to Stella's house as I went into my own. Although I was still feeling somewhat disconnected, I noticed a sense of excitement permeate my being. I could sense that my whole life was about to change. Something big was happening, something greater than what I could perceive, and I knew I needed to trust it.

I sat at the kitchen table in suspense, wondering what was going to happen next... What was Samuel going to do? And the scarier thought, what was Dad going to do? He *did* have spine—lots of it, straight and strong—and I knew my conversation with him was going to be very different from the one I'd just had with Samuel. *Not* bringing Dad into it was impossible—there was no way he would ever let me leave before he had a chance to bombard me with the words of the great prophet. And I knew he would play the guilt-card, making me feel as worthless and insignificant as he possibly could.

Not everyone knew the power my father had over me, but Samuel knew—and I had a feeling he was going to use Dad to try to guilt and shame me into staying. This tactic had always worked in the past—it was his way of manipulating me into being submissive.

I'm just going to have to be strong, I decided—suddenly feeling sick to my stomach. I could feel the fear creeping into my mind and spreading through my body. It felt black and heavy and I began to feel like I was suffocating... "God, I'm so afraid," I whispered out loud. "I want to run. Not because Samuel scares me, but because Dad does—and I don't want to face him."

As I continued to sit there, overwhelmed by fear and feeling as if it was going to kill me, I felt something stir deep inside me. It was a shimmer of light that could not be darkened by my fear—so subtle, and yet I held onto it for dear life. Somehow it inspired me to believe in myself and in my freedom. It made me feel stronger and I knew that if I focused on its warmth, I would survive Dad's judgment... *Focus on me,* it seemed to whisper. *Just focus on me.*

Later that evening, after feeding my children and getting them to bed, I retired to my own room. It was Stella's night, which meant Samuel would be with her and I would have the evening to myself. But instead of sleeping, I found myself processing my thoughts about the backlash I knew would come once the community found out that I had asked for a divorce. I wished I could leave in the morning—just hurry up and get out of town before having to face everyone. I didn't want to hear their words of advice—how to get over myself, how to cure my evil ways, how I needed to follow God's laws.

Suddenly I heard the back door open and I knew it had to be Samuel. It was unusual for him to be at my house this late on Stella's night and I wondered what he was doing here. I held my breath as I heard him walking down the hall toward our room. Then, coming into the bedroom, he said, "I told Stella you and I were having problems and she agreed to let me spend the night with you tonight." Then, sitting down on the edge of the bed, he began telling me all the reasons why divorce was wrong and unacceptable to God. I said nothing—totally uninterested as he repeated Bible quotes, which I had heard a million times before... "A woman is forever sealed to a man and divorce is a crime," he said, then continued to speak for what seemed like hours using all the fear and guilt tactics he had used in the past to get me to succumb to whatever it was he wanted.

But I did not budge—not my mind, not my heart, not my soul. No matter what he said, I silently stood firm in my decision for freedom; and he sensed it. I could feel him getting desperate. I was no longer afraid of him, and the words that were meant to manipulate me—the ones he had used so many times before—were not working. I felt his growing need to overpower me, which was both scary and liberating at the same time.

Leaning closer to me, he began caressing my arm—alluding to sex, that sacred thing that I once believed would get me to Heaven. But as soon as he touched me and the mental struggle between us got *very* real, I was more determined than ever not to allow him to make me feel like I was his servant. I was not about to fall into my old ways of unworthy thinking; but, as usual, he was determined to tame me into being submissive.

As his hands roved over me, although my mind stayed strong, I began to cry. "No," I said to him, turning away. "No!"

"Why not?" he asked, as if he didn't already know.

"Because I don't want to," I said, wishing he would go away. Far away. Forever.

"Please," he said, lifting up my nightdress and touching me.

"No, Samuel! I don't want to!" I cried out, as he forced himself into me.

Sobbing through gritted teeth, I finally gave in and let him do what he was determined to do. He was so much bigger and so much stronger than I was, and all the struggling in the world was not going to save me. But suddenly I felt the shimmer of light flow through me again—and I heard the warm, loving voice of that light speaking to me. And, as Samuel used my body, I listened to the voice that seemed to truly care about me, saying: *This is what you are standing up against. The disregard for you and your feelings, the belittling and the abuse—on you, and all the other women in this egotistical male-dominated cult—is what you are seeking freedom from. Use this experience as a reminder of what you're fighting for. Come back to it every time you question yourself or your decision to leave. It will remind you to be strong. It will inspire you to stay on the path that will take you to freedom—the freedom your soul is longing for you to experience.*

When it was finally over, when Samuel finally got off me—even though I was still choking on my own tears, I chose to let it inspire me. I wasn't free yet, and the way out still wasn't clear to me—but no longer was my resolve a flimsy "maybe tomorrow" kind of thing. As a matter of fact, that night cemented everything into place, because every part of me knew that there was no God—in any religion, on any planet, or in any Heaven—that sanctioned forced sex.

CHAPTER TWENTY-NINE

SHOWDOWN

One step forward, one step back. Two steps forward, one step back. Three steps forward, one step back... It's a strange way to travel, but it's how most of us get where we're going.

When I awoke at five o'clock the following morning, Samuel was nowhere to be found. It was unusual for him to be gone so early in the morning, but I didn't give it too much thought. I had a lot on my mind and took my time getting up and starting my morning routine.

Still dressed in my long purple nightshirt, I went about getting the children ready and off to school. After washing the dishes and making the beds, I noticed a familiar white truck pull up in front of the house. Oh my God, my mind screamed, it's Dad! Samuel must have gone to Dad's house this morning to tell him about his shameful daughter.

Dad never visited me, much less this early in the morning, and I knew exactly why he was here. Knowing I had to face him—today, this morning, right now—my entire being trembled as I ran into the front room, hysterically searching for a blanket. Finding one, I scrunched up on the couch—quickly covering up as much of myself as I could. It was as if I needed a layer of protection to shield myself psychologically from Dad and the blanket did just that. I felt like I could better hide my feelings behind the blanket in case I found myself weakening. I knew Dad would not physically hurt me, but the thought of the emotional pain I knew he was about to inflict on me scared me to death.

Dad knocked on the front door while saying to someone outside, "I'll take care of it."

His words petrified me... Take care of what?

"Come in," I said nervously, waiting for the browbeating to begin.

In walked Dad and Mama Vee... Why did he bring Mama Vee?

I knew the answer... He knows how much I love and trust her, and he's going to use the power of her influence to try to force me to change my mind.

"Good morning," I muttered.

Dad didn't waste a single second as he stood with his hands in his pockets, looking at me as if he were disgusted—saying, "What in the hell is going on, Vera? What do you think you're doing telling Samuel you want a divorce?"

Still clutching the blanket, I sat quietly for a moment trying to find the best words I could find. Words that I thought might inspire some compassion from Dad—the dad I envisioned in the mirror, looking back at me with love in his eyes.

"I'm not Amy, Dad, and I don't love him," I said.

I didn't dare tell him that I thought his religion and his Saunders prophets were full of baloney. At this point, doing so would only set me up for a losing battle that I didn't care to fight. I wanted to keep my reason for leaving as simple as possible.

Dad didn't back down. "What do you mean you don't love him? Love is a decision and in God's eyes once you have given yourself to a man you are forever his."

I knew what he meant by "given." He meant sexually—and that was reason enough to stay strong. So, with renewed resolve, I repeated, "But I don't love him!"

"Sure you do," he insisted. "You just have the spirit of the devil in you right now. That's why you want to leave. You don't need to go anywhere. Just stay here, Vera. It's the devil and we will all help you kick him in the ass. You have no reason to be feeling this way. Samuel has provided you with a home, food and clothing."

I thought about how Dad had struggled to provide these things for my mother and all her children. And all his other wives, and all their children... Probably thinking the same thing I was thinking, he added, "You have no justifiable reason to want to leave."

"But Dad, I want to know things for myself. I want to make sense of my own life."

"That is ridiculous," he said, raising his voice a little. "There is no divorce in God's eyes, and you will be turned over to the buffetings of Satan if you go through with this."

On the other couch, Mama Vee sat quietly, listening as Dad spoke. I was sure that if she didn't love him, she would be on my side and she would understand me completely.

In his preaching voice, Dad continued talking about Jerome, the prophet, and celestial marriage. "This is the greatest blessing God ever gave his people and if you go against it, you will have to face God on judgment day. You have no excuse, Vera. I raised you better than this and you know it."

Fed by hot air, my thoughts sizzled. The Spitfire snarled, jumping up and standing strong inside me... *I know better than what?* Oh, I really didn't want to go in this direction, but before I had time to think about what I was going to say, the words spit themselves out—demanding answers, "Why did God give me a brain to figure things out if I'm supposed to just do whatever you and your prophets say I should do? Why would God give me the ability to think if he didn't want me to think for myself?"

A sob erupting from somewhere deep in my soul created its own kind of pause, then the fire took over again. "Why, Dad? Why couldn't God just make me without a brain? It would be so much easier."

Tears poured from my eyes, but I was on the road to freedom and I was determined to stay on it. My voice rising with the fire, I added belligerently, "You would never have to worry about me straying from the path, and Samuel could have the perfect concubine. If I had no brain and no ability to think for myself, he could program me like a computer to walk, talk and be exactly how he wants me to be! He could even program me to go directly to Heaven if he wanted to. So, why? Why do I have the ability to think and feel for myself?"

Dad stared at me with a blank look in his eyes. Suddenly empty, as if he had no answer for my outburst and as though he had never thought about it this way before.

Sensing that perhaps I was getting somewhere with this conversation, I continued, "Listen, Dad, if you can take away my ability to think for myself and if you can take away my ability to feel, I will stay. Tell me what to do to get rid of those two things—my thoughts and my feelings—and I'll do it. I'll stay."

The silence that followed my words was thick as molasses. Dad glared at me.

I, too, was shocked that I had dared to talk to him this way. I wasn't sure where my words had come from, but I liked them! They had stopped Dad dead in his tracks—left him speechless, totally obliterating the fear, guilt and shame cards he had pulled from his bag of polygamist-tricks—and, probably for the first time in his life, his vengeful God could not argue with my God.

He was quiet for a few minutes—looking as though he was deep in thought—then finally said, "Vera, I believe you must have some kind of chemical imbalance that you need to address. You have no reason to leave."

Noticing the distant look in his eyes, I realized he would never understand or agree with me. He had dedicated his whole life to his church and his religion. For him to understand me, he would first need to understand himself and his own wives—what they went through, how they felt, what they would say if they weren't so afraid—and it was painfully clear he wasn't willing to do that... All the years I had spent living in fear of this man flashed before my eyes and I realized that I had never once dared to confront him.

Angry as I was, I felt my understanding grow... I could see he had a lot of fears and that he had raised and governed me with the terrifying beliefs he could not free himself from. His God was to be feared, and he continued to drive that point home for the next two hours.

I sat quietly, knowing I would never get his blessing and quite frankly I didn't care. I only felt stronger as I sat there, letting his words turn to dust.

Dad had somewhere to be and eventually decided to leave, but Mama Vee stayed for a while longer. As soon as Dad walked out the door she came over and sat facing me on the couch. She put both her hands on my shoulders and stared deep into my teary eyes. "I love you, darling," she said, as tears streamed down her face too. Then she wrapped her arms around me and hugged me for the longest time.

Although she wasn't saying anything, I could sense her deep, unconditional love and acceptance. Unlike Dad, she had heard what I said about Amy, and she understood my feelings about Samuel. I knew she understood. She didn't want me to leave either because she also believed in Jerome's teachings—but I knew she believed in me and how I was feeling. Without saying a word she had given me her blessing, a blessing that my dad would never be capable of giving me because it went against his radical belief in a polygamist cult where women must obey their husbands at all costs—even if it cost them their own souls.

CHAPTER THIRTY

U.S. BOUND

For those who look with their hearts, where there is no way a way suddenly appears.

The dawn was just beginning to break as I said goodbye to the Saunders colony. A place that I once believed was the only place on earth where God lived. A place where I once thought that I would be given the keys to Heaven by obeying God's celestial law. A place that I never wanted to return to.

A few weeks ago, I had no idea how I was going to get from where I was to where I wanted to be but strangely, out of nowhere, a way suddenly appeared... Many members of the cult (and of my family) were construction workers in different areas of the United States, and a few of them had returned to Mexico for Elise's wedding. Oddly enough, their returning opened the door to my leaving, and I quickly made arrangements to ride back to the States with them after the wedding.

My decision to leave my marriage, the cult and the country was absolutely against the wishes of my husband and my father. Samuel prayed to his polygamist God that I would quickly come to my senses and return a repented woman. Meanwhile, Dad prayed to his polygamist God that I would be spared from the buffetings of Satan and asked that I be healed of my supposed "chemical imbalance." They both believed that because I had no work experience, I would not be able to support myself or my children, and that it wouldn't be long before I would come crawling back, begging for forgiveness.

"God is going to humble you," Dad warned. But I didn't listen to him because I was sure the opposite was true—that my God was going to be proud of me. I didn't know how I was going to take care of my children, financially or emotionally, but I was willing to die trying. It would be a cold day in hell before I ever gave up on my freedom and returned, and I was determined to do whatever it took to live life on my own terms.

A family member agreed to let me stay at his home in the northern part of the U.S., and I remained there for the next few months. I applied for many jobs but with no work history, I was never hired. So, intent on finding a way to continue living in the U.S., I decided to start a business doing the only thing I knew how to do which was to clean houses. My business took off like wildfire and within a few months I was supporting myself.

After six months I hired my first employee. And, as I continued to grow my business and raise my three children, I also went back to school. I loved learning and wanted to do everything I could to enhance my newfound sense of self-worth. And I did!

I was bound and determined to create a future for myself and my children, so I worked hard and for eight years I never took a day off. My cleaning business went on to become amazingly successful and is now mostly owned and operated by my grown children.

I have always been fascinated with health (physical *and* mental), which led me to invest in educating myself in these areas, which subsequently inspired me to invest my time and energy in health-related businesses. Perhaps it was my desire to not only help myself but to help others as well, that kept me going in this new direction.

Intense determination is a powerful force to be reckoned with, but to say my transition into a new life in a new country was easy, would not be true. It was not easy, and there were times (especially the first few months after leaving Mexico) that I struggled with the loss of my relationship with Amy's children. I had to come to terms with the fact that I could not maintain a relationship with them and, at the same time, separate myself from their father and the cult he was part of. This was very, very hard on me, and I spent many nights crying myself to sleep. I missed them so much and I knew they were missing me too, but I did what I had to do to stay strong—which was something I had learned to do well in the cult. Deep in my soul, I also carried the knowing that the years I had been with them, and the many happy moments we had shared, would forever be engraved in my heart—and it was this "knowing" that brought me comfort during the hardest of times.

At the beginning, different members of the cult (and certain members of my family) tried to convince me to come back. Harassing phone calls were a never-ending story. Samuel even made a special trip to visit me, as did my father, for a final attempt at saving my soul from hell. But hard as it sometimes was, I was in heaven and I was never going back to polygamist hell. My God loved me. My God allowed me to honor my feelings. My God encouraged me to be proud of being a woman. And my God did not require me to marry my sister's husband or any woman's husband in order to be allowed into Heaven.

CHAPTER THIRTY-ONE

BACK TO THE PROLOGUE

January 15, 2013

Finding Samuel's face among the mourners at my father's funeral, my eyes quickly move away from his as fear moves through my body. I search the faces of many of my siblings, hoping to find one pair of eyes to draw strength from. But one set of eyes after another all hold so much sadness and seem to have no strength to give. I can see each pair of eyes carrying their own pain and suffering. Some, not as sad as others, and some with a sadness so deep that it feels like I'm sinking into a weeping shadow that has replaced what was once a shining soul.

It is more than I can bare, and I silently begin to sob. Feeling their misery stirs the memory of my own—as well as all the questions that remain unanswered in my heart... How could such a religious man with so much faith in God instill so much fear in his offspring? Is not faith the absence of fear? How could my father have been so focused on receiving the gift of eternal salvation that he completely missed out on the gift of a loving relationship with so many of us? How could he have devoted so much of his time to upholding the cult and preaching about the destruction of the United

States and yet be ignorant of the destruction of the hearts of so many of his children?

As tears poured from my heart, the fear began to subside, and in its place came a feeling of calm. I remembered that I was free of it all and had nothing to fear. I was no longer the little girl who was afraid of the wrath of her father's polygamist God, and Samuel no longer had the power to fill me with guilt for wanting to be loved. I had changed—and by changing what I believed, I had changed my entire life.

My eyes quickly move back to the coffin that holds my father's lifeless body and I know that he too has now changed. Death has changed him. He no longer lives in the illusion of his belief system because he no longer has a physical body with a rampant mind that thrives on fear. He has transitioned into being only Spirit; and if Spirit is love, then all he could give me now was love in its purest form.

All the judgment, shame, guilt and fear were gone from him, and it was amazing to feel this type of love from my father. I had longed for it since the day I was born, and I could now feel it embracing me. It didn't matter that he had to die for me to experience it. What mattered was that I could now live knowing that from Spirit he truly did love me—and that all those loveless years of being his daughter, I was on a path that eventually taught me the importance of loving and honoring myself.

As I continue to gaze at the coffin, I realize that without the lifeless man within it I would not be the woman I am today—and an overwhelming feeling of gratitude engulfs me. *Thank you, Dad,* is all I hear my heart saying. *Thank you!*

Suddenly I feel a nudge from my sister who is quietly standing next to me. It is a warning nudge, letting me know that Samuel is making his way over to me. I can see him out of the corner of my eye, and I try not to feel nervous. Once again, I remind myself that there is nothing left to fear. It has been ten years since I've seen him, and nothing is the same between us. My eyes make contact with his as he gets closer, and I am determined to extend only love and to hold myself in a place of love as well, no matter what he might say.

"Thank you for the way you raised my children," he said, as we both reached out and gave each other a hug. And then came the tears. Shared tears. Mine, a release of deep gratitude for the blessing of finally experiencing his presence without fear. And it felt as if his tears were an outpouring of forgiveness—washing the slate clean, pardoning me for leaving him and the cult without having to put it into words (although I had no way of knowing that for sure). I also wasn't sure if he had meant that he was grateful for the way I had raised our three children, or for the way I had helped raise Amy's children, but either way I felt his sincerity.

In that moment, I believed that my departure from the cult and from him may have caused him to "look a little deeper," and there was every possibility that it might also have caused ripple effects of goodness and growth for his entire family. Once again, an unexpected bolt of gratitude struck me, followed by a burst of pride as the thought that I may have done something courageously wonderful—not just for myself but for many others as well—wound its way through my mind. And, to this day, I carry that belief with me. The belief that I can and do make a difference in my own life and in the lives of others.

AUTHOR'S NOTE

God works in mysterious ways, is something I heard throughout my childhood—never believing that I would be included, as a female, in any of his bigger plans. But now I see that I was mistaken, and I feel so blessed to have been created by a Creator whose love is extended to all his creations equally—and that we are all part of the "bigger plan."

After many years of inner-work and self-reflection, I now believe that the basis for all life is freedom, and God's biggest quest is to experience joy and love through me. I do not believe that my circumstances were meant to define me. Rather, they were meant to reveal me, and they have. They have revealed me to be more than I ever dreamed of being. They have revealed me to be pure love, that which God is made of. A love that is eternal, unconditional, and conquers all fear. And, today, because of that unwavering belief, Dad no longer scares me, and God no longer scares me, for I know without a doubt that I Am Love. Forever, I AM LOVE.

ABOUT THE AUTHOR

Born into a polygamist cult in Mexico in 1971, Vera LaRee was one of fifty-seven children her father had with his eleven wives. Constantly told that women were inferior to men and God was to be feared, from an early age she experienced manipulation, brainwashing, and sexual violation. Married off to her deceased sister's husband at the age of sixteen, she helped raise her sister's children and gave birth to three of her own while the manipulation and fear continued. But it all changed when the seed of a single idea she read in a hidden book slowly started taking root.

In 2002, Vera mustered up the courage to escape to the United States with her three children, a suitcase of clothes and $500 to her name. Determined not to return to the cult she was born into, she started a successful cleaning service, then passionately immersed herself in the study of psychology and all things spiritual.

Today, holding certifications in Therapeutic Coaching, NLP, Positive Psychology, HNLP and personal training, she lives the life she chooses to live and devotes her time to helping others break free of their mental bondage.

For more information, please visit: www.veralaree.com

Made in the USA
Monee, IL
26 May 2020